Shattering Black Male Stereotypes

Eradicating the 10 Most Destructive
Media-Generated Illusions About Black Men

Published by Creation Publishing Group LLC
www.creationpublishing.com

© 2018 Michael Taylor

ISBN # **978-0-9969487-4-6**

Library of Congress Number # 2017914648

Published and printed in the United States of America.

In loving memory of:

Philando Castille
My heart is still broken
Rest In Paradise

Table of Contents

Acknowledgements

To my source

First, foremost and always, I must acknowledge the Divine Energy and Intelligence that created and is still creating this amazing Universe that we live in. As I write these words I am filled with optimism and gratitude for this amazing gift called life. I can never find the words to fully express the joy and love I have in my heart as a result of my connection with you, so I will simply say that I love you more than love itself. Thank you for the gifts you have given me and I am committed to using them to be in service to you by making the world a better place.

Who I am is your gift to me. What I make of myself is my gift back to you!

To all men of color:

I would like to acknowledge you for being willing to break free from the negative cultural and societal stereotypes that attempt to define who we are. I acknowledge you for succeeding against the odds. Your willingness to overcome the multiplicity of challenges you are faced with on a daily basis fills me with great pride. I acknowledge you for the intelligence, courage, patience, perseverance, and most of all for your faith in yourself to believe that you are the master of your own destiny. The time has come for us to no longer feel victimized by society but to be empowered by embracing our own authentic power that will ensure that we become victorious in all areas of our lives.

It's our time! We got this!

Introduction

I would like to begin this book with a very bold statement. This statement is going to set the context for the entire book and it's important for you to grasp the implications of its message because once you complete this book you should have a more optimistic and inspired view of yourself and the world around you.

So, are you ready? Are you ready to accept the truth that will set you free and propel you to live the life of your dreams? Are you ready to move past any obstacle or challenge you may be dealing with right now and stop struggling with your life and start enjoying it?

If you're truly ready, read and understand this statement:

"You currently have everything you need right now inside of you to live an extraordinary life."

This is the simple truth that will set you free. Rest assured that there is a divine intelligence that resides in you, and if you are courageous enough to uncover it nothing will be impossible for you.

To confirm this, let me share a brief history of my life and how I discovered this divine intelligence within me. I was born in the inner-city projects of Corpus Christi, Texas, to a single mom with six kids. We were the poster children for poverty back in the sixties. At the age of seventeen, I was a high school dropout, who was statistically destined for failure. Despite those odds, I was able to climb the corporate ladder and was living the American Dream at the tender age of twenty-three. I was married with two kids, had purchased my first home, and was able to take nice vacations. By society's standards, I was successful.

At the age of twenty-nine, my American Dream turned into the American nightmare as I went through a divorce, bankruptcy, foreclosure, and a deep state of depression. During this dark period of my life, I made a commitment to myself that I was going to turn everything around and no matter what it took I was going to be happy again. It was this commitment I made to myself that propelled me on an inner journey of transformation, and it changed everything.

As a result of my inner journey of transformation, I was able to turn my life around, and I must admit that I am happier right now than I've ever been before. I'm currently happily married (15 years), an entrepreneur, author (6 books), motivational speaker, and a radio and TV host who has committed his life to supporting others to transform their lives from the inside out.

As a man who happens to be black, I believe I have a

responsibility to speak directly to black men through this book to let them know that despite current external challenges, it is possible for any man of color to create a rewarding and fulfilling life.

On the outside looking in it may appear that the challenges facing black men are insurmountable. Racism, police brutality, high incarceration rates, poverty, and a host of other challenges lie before us. Far too many people have become apathetic or simply feel powerless to do something that changes things. Too many people have simply resigned and surrendered to the idea that there is a war against black men and nothing can be done about it.

But there are some of us who choose to be more optimistic and proactive in our approach to addressing the challenges that black men face. We believe the key to resolving our challenges will not be through political, legislative, or even religious means. We understand the negative "external" media-generated narrative about black men is inaccurate, and the only way to create concrete solutions to our problems is to change the "internal" narrative black men hold about themselves.

And this is the reason I've written this book. I want to change your mind set about what it means to be a man who happens to be black. I want you to recognize that the divine intelligence I mentioned earlier is within you, and when you access it you gain the keys to your own inner kingdom. This is the key to your success. To change the way you view yourself from the inside out.

By recognizing the ten most negative media-generated illusions I will be sharing in this book and not being consistent with them, you will then have the tools to live the life you were born to live and be in control of your own destiny.

Good luck!

My Intention

My intention for this book is simple. I want to dispel the negative media generated stereotypes about black men. To do this I must begin by having a conversation with you. That's right - this book is written specifically for *you*. It doesn't matter what color you are or what your religious orientation might be. It doesn't matter if you're young or old, rich or poor, gay or straight, republican or democrat. If you're a human being (or an alien from another planet) and you're reading this book, I can assure you that the messages contained within are for you.

You see, I do not believe in accidents. The fact that you are reading these words right now is confirmation for me that this is a divine appointment. We have come together to engage in a conversation that I believe will change your perception of black men.

It just so happens that I am an irrepressible optimist with a passion for the impossible, and I believe this conversation will give you reason for optimism - not just for black men, but for all of humanity.

It is my belief that there has never been a better time to be alive on this planet, and I also believe that the future is filled with infinite possibilities for anyone who is willing to take control of their own destiny.

Unfortunately, there are too many people who have accepted that black men are somehow different, and in too many cases, *less than* other men. By the time you finish reading this book, my hope is that you will see that we are no different than any other group of men, and despite what the media shows you, we are positioned for unprecedented levels of success in America and the world abroad.

So, let me welcome you to this conversation in which I dispel the negative media-generated stereotypes about black men, and in doing so, I believe we can move forward in creating solutions to the majority of challenges facing our world today.

Welcome to the conversation!

Reasons for Optimism

If you conducted a survey about the status of America and asked participants if they felt positive or negative about the future of this country, I believe most would say they were pessimistic. One reason for their pessimism can be traced to the fact that our current president has promoted the idea that America is in steady decline and he is going to bring the country back from the brink of destruction. His slogan *"Make America Great Again"* implies that the country isn't already great (although I believe it is and always has been), and is in need of his help. If you combine his pessimistic rhetoric and beliefs about America with the constant barrage of negative media stories, it isn't too difficult to understand why so many people feel so pessimistic.

So, let me begin by asking you: Are you optimistic or pessimistic about the future of America?

Before you answer the question, let me assure you of one thing: **it is not my intention to try to tell you what to think.**

My job is to simply **challenge you to think**. As you are reading this book, my intention is to challenge your beliefs and assumptions about the world we live in and to share my points of view and beliefs. These are simply my beliefs and perceptions about this amazing Universe we live in and it is your responsibility to come to your own conclusions about the content I will be sharing with you.

To get the most out of this book I recommend that you treat the content like a new pair of shoes. For some, the information will be too uncomfortable and will not be accepted. For others, it will take a little getting used to, but they will choose to carry some of the ideas presented here and allow themselves to grow into them. For others, the content will be just perfect. They will be open-minded and comfortable with the message I'm sharing, and they will choose to accept the ideas and apply them to their lives to not only improve their own way of living but to support others in doing the same. It doesn't matter which category you fall in to. If you're still reading, it tells me you are at least willing to consider some of these ideas, and I am absolutely certain you will gain valuable insights if you are willing to finish reading this book.

So, let's get back to the question: *Are you optimistic or pessimistic about the future of America?*

For me, the answer is simple. I am absolutely optimistic about the future! Not just for America, but for the entire world. As a matter of fact, I would say that I believe there has never been a better time to be alive on the planet than right now. I'm so excited about the future I can barely contain myself!

Amazingly, very few people share my optimism (especially if you happen to be black). As a result of my optimism, I have been attacked, criticized, and vilified for being *out of touch* with the challenges facing black men. I have been called a wide variety of names and accused of being a sellout, just because I simply choose to have an optimistic outlook on life.

Going back to my new pair of shoes analogy, I completely understand why some people disagree with my optimistic outlook. I realize that this goes against the prevailing narrative that black men are an endangered species, and this can definitely make some people feel uncomfortable. For others, it may appear that I am insensitive to the challenges facing black men, and it may feel as if I'm denying the fact that racism and discrimination still exist. For others, it might seem as if I am in complete denial of the atrocities of the past inflicted on black people in this country. And then there will be some who are extremely comfortable with my assertion and will completely agree with my optimistic outlook.

So what about you? Are the shoes too tight for you? Are you willing to at least try them on and see how you like them? Or are you strutting around with the new pair of shoes saying how much you like them and how glad you are that you purchased them?

Remember, my job isn't to tell you **what** to think but to **challenge** you to think. What are you thinking right now?

Now that you know what I think and how I feel about the future, I'd like to share why I think and feel this way.

First of all, I have to acknowledge my mom for implanting such a positive outlook in me. If there is such a thing as an optimism gene I definitely picked it up from her. Despite all the challenges of being a single mom with six kids with only a high school education, my mom has always been an optimist. No matter what adversity she faced, she somehow found a way to turn lemons into lemonade.

As I reflect back over my mom's life, living in the inner-city projects, being on government assistance, and sometimes working three jobs just to make ends meet, I am absolutely in awe of how she never complained about anything and never allowed her circumstances to cause her to become pessimistic. Without question, she is the primary reason for my optimism.

The second reason I am so optimistic is because of a lesson I learned from my grandfather. I'd like to share the introduction I wrote to one of my previous books *Black Men Rock ~ 10 Keys To Empower Black Men To Live Extraordinary Lives* (2013). This introduction summarizes the lessons I learned from him and will give you a glimpse of his wisdom.

Introduction

When I was approximately 10 years old, I remember a conversation I had with my grandfather about race. I'll begin by letting you know that I believe he only had an 8th-grade education, yet he was one of the smartest men I've ever known. As I reflect back on all of the books I've read, the seminars I've attended, and the audio programs I've listened to over the years, I realize that the most important lessons about life I learned from him, and he was by far my greatest teacher.

He was a deeply religious man who never preached or tried to tell me what to believe about God, but he always made sure that I understood the importance of believing in a power greater than myself. He was definitely a man of deep faith with a deep spiritual connection to the God of his understanding.

During our conversation, I asked him why God allowed Black people to suffer so much. As a child, I noticed the atrocities inflicted upon Black people, and I really wanted to understand why God allowed them to happen.

As he looked at me with his loving, caring eyes, he could tell that I was a little upset with the question, and he caringly embraced me and instilled his deep wisdom.

"First of all, Michael, you must understand that God never makes mistakes. It's difficult for us to truly know God's purpose for things sometimes, but I trust in God's plan, and I know that ultimately His plan is always perfect. Since I believe in God's perfect plan, I must accept it, even when I can't fully understand it. I believe God has a perfect plan for Black people, and though it may appear that God has deserted us, He hasn't, and He is always there for us.

"The key is for you to recognize that you must always play the hand that is dealt you. If God made you Black, then that is the hand God dealt you, and it is your responsibility to play that hand. Remember, God does not make mistakes! The most important thing to remember is that your success depends on how you play the hand that you were dealt. Never question the hand; simply learn to play it to the best of your ability."

If I had to sum up the key to my own success, I would sum it up with those words of wisdom from my grandfather:

"You must always play the hand that you were dealt, and if God made you Black, then that is the hand God dealt you!"

Fortunately for me, I embraced these words of wisdom at a very young age, which has allowed me to overcome some seemingly insurmountable obstacles and build the life of my dreams. As a result of accepting this truth, I can say with absolute certainty and conviction that as a Black man, I have never felt that the color of my skin was a disadvantage. In no way have I ever felt or believed that being Black was a negative or bad thing. I have always believed that it was an asset, not a liability, and this way of thinking has empowered me to accomplish some pretty amazing things in my life. I have simply played my hand to the best of my ability.

As I see it, one of the greatest challenges we have as Black men is to recognize that being Black is not a disadvantage. This does not mean that racism, discrimination and a myriad of other challenges don't exist; it simply means that you have to accept the hand you were dealt and learn how to play that hand to the best of your ability.

There are some people who believe that Black men are an endangered species and that there is nothing that can be done to stop the eradication of the Black male species. I, however, do not believe this nonsense, and it is my belief that Black men are doing better than ever and that the future is extremely bright for Black men. I do not deny the challenges; I simply believe that there has never been an obstacle placed before Black men that we haven't overcome.

When I think about things like slavery, discrimination, prejudice, ignorance, and the negative media images of Black men, I don't feel victimized; I personally feel inspired and empowered. I feel inspired that I belong to a group of men that epitomizes faith, determination, perseverance, persistence, and courage. I feel inspired because I recognize that despite all of the obstacles placed in front of us, we have found a way to thrive and flourish in a country that seemed to do everything in its power to keep us from succeeding; therefore, I stand proud as a man who happens to be Black, and I believe the best is yet to come.

Our challenge is to change our mindset from that of victim to that of victor. We Are Not Victims! Without question, we have been victimized, but that does not mean that we have to remain victims because what happens to you isn't as important as what you do with what happens to you. Instead of feeling victimized, recognize that you are victorious despite what may have happened to you if you choose to have a victorious mindset.

We must embrace the idea that we are filled with unlimited potential and that it is our responsibility to access our innate magnificence and personal power. The time has come for us to begin empowering and supporting each other in reaching our full potential and to be willing to share our wisdom with others to help them overcome their own struggles. "Reach one and teach one" must become our motto, and when we do this, we will begin to see the eradication of the majority of the social ills that currently plague our communities.

And most importantly, it's time for us to recognize that the "struggle" is over. Being caught in the "struggle" is an antiquated mindset that will keep you trapped in mediocrity and the victim mentality. Yes, there are still challenges, but the doors of opportunity are wide open for those of us who are willing to walk through them and live the life of our dreams. Struggle is a choice. My suggestion is that you simply choose not to believe that your life has to be a struggle, and it won't be.

This also means that we must eliminate the idea that society and white people are conspiring against us. It is my contention that the overwhelming majority of white people are definitely not racist and conspiring to keep us down. Most of them are supportive and caring and open-minded and want the same things that we do. We want to love and be loved, we want to feel that we make a difference, and we want peace of mind and a sense of purpose. Isn't that what you really want out of life?

Of course it is; it's what all human beings strive for. No longer can we blame white people or society for us not accomplishing these things. If you want to be loved, to make a difference in the world, and to have inner peace and a sense of purpose, it is completely up to you. You simply have to believe that you're capable of attaining these things and then get started in making them happen.

As we move into 2013, let's declare that it is the year of infinite possibilities. Make a commitment to yourself that you are going to live an extraordinary life and that there is nothing that can keep you from it. Know that you already have everything you need to make this a reality for yourself but that it is definitely going to take a considerable amount of effort on your part. It may be difficult, but I can promise you that it will be worth it.

My commitment to you is to share my experience and wisdom to support you on your journey. The good news is that you do not have to do this alone. There are lots of other men and women who will support you if you are willing to seek the support.

This book is my attempt to share some wisdom and knowledge with you that can encourage and motivate you to create your best life ever. If I can overcome seemingly insurmountable obstacles to live an extraordinary life, then I know that you can, too. You just have to be willing to take the first step, and I believe if you are reading this right now, you have done just that. Congratulations on taking the first step to living an extraordinary life!

I look forward to seeing you along the way!

Never forget: "You must always play the hand that you were dealt, and if God made you Black, then that is the hand God dealt you, and rest assured that it is a positive hand!"

No matter what color you are, it's perfect. Just play the hand you were dealt to the best of your ability, and you, too, will live an extraordinary life!

~~~~~~~~~~~~

Fortunately for me, my mom and my grandfather laid the foundation for my optimism. I feel truly blessed to have incorporated a positive mental attitude at a very young age and the wisdom I learned from them definitely contributed to my success.

The next reason for my optimism is my own personal experience. Back in the sixties, I remember listening to the grownups talk about white people. In a lot of cases, the things they said could have caused me to dislike white people, but my experience taught me otherwise. Despite the racial tension of the sixties I had a few white friends whom I really liked and cared about. I didn't see them as white - I simply saw them as my friends, which confirms a simple truth: people aren't born racist. It is learned behavior, and if it is learned it can be unlearned. My early childhood experiences convinced me that I could be friends with anybody, regardless of what color they were.

As I moved up to junior high I had my first experience with blatant racism. There were racially motivated fights in school and I had my life threatened for falling in love with a girl who happened to be white. Despite the fights and rejection for the color of my skin, I held firm to the belief that most people weren't racist and I simply made a choice to not buy into the hate or belief in separation.

By the time I got to high school, I was completely comfortable interacting with people of all races. I went to an affluent, predominately white, high school and created some friendships that I still have to this day. Each friendship I developed solidified my belief that black people and white people are all the same and there was no reason for me to accept the belief that we were in any way different.

Even today, I have friends who happen to be white whom I love dearly and would even trust them with my life. Men who know me at my deepest level, who have loved and accepted me for the man that I am, not the *black man* the media tries to portray me as.

As a man who happens to be black, I really resonate with what Booker T. Washington once said: *"Success is not to be measured by what one accomplishes in life. Success should be measured by the obstacles one overcomes while trying to succeed.*" As I reflect back over my life and all the obstacles I've overcome, I recognize another thing that fuels my optimism is the fact that I've overcome some seemingly insurmountable obstacles in my life and that I was able to do so with only a GED confirms that anything is possible if you set your mind to it.

Another reason for my optimism is my own observations about the progress black people have made in this country. I definitely do not deny the challenges black men face and I am acutely aware that racism and discrimination are real and in too many cases creates unnecessary challenges that are difficult to overcome. I am also aware that the justice system is unfair, and far too many young black men have had their lives devastated by unfair court systems and inadequate representation. I know that racial profiling exists and too many black men are still being judged simply because of the color of their skin.

For the most part, I know that the media will generally focus on everything wrong with the world. We are constantly bombarded with negative images filled with excessive violence and dysfunction, which creates the perception that the world is a terrible place to be in.

If you pay attention to the media, you might even conclude that most black men are baggy pants-wearing, gun-toting gangsters who objectify women and dress like rappers. You might also conclude that the majority of young black men are incarcerated and are a liability to society. These negative images generated by our media are what fuel the perception that black men are an endangered species, and I simply do not buy into that negative perception.

On the flip side of that, you may also notice that the media will definitely showcase black male athletes and entertainers. Which for the most part is a good thing, but the bad news is it implies that all black men are only capable of dancing, singing, and playing sports. What you may not be aware of is that we are CEOs of billion-dollar companies. We are leaders in medicine and surgery. We're brilliant scientists and intellectual thinkers, and we're also powerful leaders and communicators.

As a matter of fact, there is no segment of society that does not have a black male presence: we are Chemists and Engineers, Authors and Psychologists, Mayors and Senators, Realtors and Contractors. And the list goes on. These are examples of the successes we've attained, and they provide me with proof that we have definitely made progress in America, which further substantiates my optimism.

I would like to share some statistics compiled by filmmaker and author Janks Morton. Mr. Morton has dedicated his life to dispelling the negative media-generated stereotypes about black men, and he has done extensive research to debunk a lot of this negativity specifically about the status of black men in America. According to Mr. Morton, here are some statistics that show how much progress black males have made between the year 2000 and 2012. In those years, black males receiving their High School Diploma or GED increased by 8.22%.

During this period, the high school dropout rate decreased by 45.75%, and college enrollment increased by 34.61%, while the incarceration rate decreased by 21.71%. The total number of black males in college increased by 78%, and the number of black males receiving a college degree increased by 23.46%.

I generally dislike statistics because they can be misconstrued to support any point of view, but these statistics resonate with me and I firmly believe in their validity. I believe that we are on a trajectory to experience unprecedented levels of success in the future, and it is our responsibility to continue these trends and ensure that every black male in this country has the opportunity to reach his fullest potential.

I've heard some talking heads on television who say black people aren't doing enough to resolve the challenges within our communities. To which I reply, *we have **always** worked toward solutions* yet the media will seldom show the solutions and progress we've made. There are literally hundreds of grassroots movements that are working to address the challenges facing young black males, and I'd like to take a moment to share just a few of them.

100 Black Men of America (www.100blackmen.org)

The 100 improves the quality of life for the communities we serve. Mentoring is the core service delivery of The 100, the largest network of African American male mentors in the nation. We influence and transform the lives of underrepresented and disenfranchised youth, with a focus on African American youth. Through our platform of Mentoring The 100 Way®Across A

Lifetime, we provide programmatic services in education, health and wellness, economic empowerment and leadership development, which makes a fundamental difference in the lives of the youth we touch and the communities we serve.

The Black Man Can Institute
(www.theblackmancan.org)

TheBlackManCan Institute is a mentoring program designed to uplift, empower, educate, and motivate young men of color.

This organization was founded by educator Brandon Frame and has grown to receive several accolades for the wonderful work they do with youth.

Urban Prep Academy (www.urbanprep.org)

Urban Prep Academies is a nonprofit organization operating a network of all-male public schools, including the country's first charter high school for boys. Urban Prep's mission is to provide a high-quality and comprehensive college-preparatory educational experience to young men that results in graduates succeeding in college. The schools are a direct response to the urgent need to reverse abysmal graduation and college completion rates among boys in urban centers. While most of Urban Prep students come to the schools from economically disadvantaged households and behind in many subject areas, Urban Prep remains committed to preparing all of its students for college and life.

My Brothers Keeper Alliance (www.mbkalliance.org)

This organization was launched during President

Barack Obama's time in office. It is still a focal point of the Obama Foundation's commitment to empowering young men of color, and I'm certain it will continue to have a positive impact on the lives of young black males.

From their website:

We believe every young person deserves equal opportunity to achieve success and prosperity, regardless of circumstance. Our vision is to make this a reality for all of our nation's boys and young men of color, each and every one of whom is critical to our collective success. By realizing this vision, we are creating a brighter, more promising future not just for our boys and young men of color, but for our country as a whole.

BMR Academy (www.bmracademy.com)

This is the academy I founded to provide men of color with personal growth and development tools to support them in living extraordinary lives. It is filled with resources designed specifically for men of color and helps them address the unique psychological and emotional aspect of who they are.

~~~~~~~~~~~~~~

These are just a few of the organizations that are dedicated to empowering men of color to succeed. The list does not include the hundreds of teachers, coaches, ministers, activists, and entrepreneurs who are working tirelessly to build a better life for our youth. These organizations fuel my optimism because I recognize how important their work is, and it is through them we begin creating concrete solutions to the challenges we face.

So the next time you hear a talking head saying we aren't doing anything to resolve the challenges in our communities, simply dismiss their comments, join one of these organizations, and donate your time and money to help them help our youth.

~ ~ ~ ~ ~ ~ ~ ~ ~ ~ ~ ~ ~

If you take the time to really think about it, this country has actually come a very long way in a short amount of time. In my short lifetime (56 years), it has gone from not letting people of color vote, to actually voting for a man of color to run the country. For a country that is only 241 years old (at the time of this writing), America has evolved into what I consider the greatest country on the planet. Even as I think about the horrible atrocities that have been inflicted (and in too many ways are still being inflicted) on people of color, I still hold the belief that our best days are ahead of us and not behind us.

Of course, none of this would be possible without the brave men and women who fought so valiantly for equal rights. Men and women who sacrificed their lives to ensure that America lives up to its creed of *"all men being created equal."* Men and women who are still being ostracized for wanting to make the country better. And yet they persist. Which reminds me of my favorite quote from Steve Jobs:

> *"Here's to the crazy ones. The misfits, the rebels, the round pegs in the square holes. The ones who see things*

differently. They aren't fond of rules and they have no respect for the status quo. You can quote them, disagree with them, glorify or vilify them. But the one thing you can't do is ignore them, because they change things. They push the human race forward. And while some may see them as the crazy ones, we see genius. Because the people who are crazy enough to think they can change the world are the ones who do."

The first time I watched the video of this quote it brought me to tears. There was a part of me that resonated so deeply with it that I intuitively knew the quote was speaking directly to me. I have always felt like one of the crazy ones. The ones who see things differently. And I am definitely crazy enough to believe that I can change the world.

And that is the reason I am so optimistic about the future. I'm crazy enough to believe that I can change it.

The Origin of Stereotypes

The term stereotype can be defined as *"a widely held but fixed and oversimplified image or idea of a particular type of person or thing."*

Or: *"A generalization, usually exaggerated or oversimplified and often offensive, that is used to describe or distinguish a group."*

I would like to give you my definition of stereotype and as you read this book use this definition as a reference. *"A stereotype is an unconscious, subconscious belief that we hold in our minds about a person or a thing."*

As you're reading this book I want you to remember this quote by Danny Iny (CEO/Mirasee):

> *"Belief is about that feeling in your core that something is true... and a commitment to upholding that truth through your thoughts and actions. Our beliefs drive our actions, often without any conscious thought. That's why understanding the beliefs of those around us is so important - it makes it a whole lot easier to know what to*

expect from them, and whether their deep values align with yours."

In summary, your beliefs literally create your reality. As mentioned, *"a stereotype is an unconscious, subconscious belief that we hold in our minds about a person or a thing."* As long as we hold a belief in our minds and hearts, that belief will shape how we think and behave.

To fully understand how stereotypes are formed, it's important to understand how the human mind works. According to Dr. Bruce Lipton, author of the amazing book, *The Biology of Belief*, the mind actually has two parts: the *conscious* mind and the *subconscious* mind. A great metaphor to explain how it works is an iceberg. If you look at an iceberg in the ocean you will only see a small portion of it above the water, but did you know that in some cases 90% of the iceberg is actually *below* the surface? This is how the mind works. The top 10% is your conscious mind, and the lower 90% is your subconscious mind. What is really fascinating is that the subconscious mind is actually **1000 times more powerful** than the conscious mind when it comes to influencing your behavior.

Dr. Lipton explained it this way;

"When we are born, we are completely conscious of all the external stimuli that we interact with. As children, we process primarily through our feelings without judgment or thought about the situation. In other words, we use our hearts, not our minds, to interpret everything around us. Our feelings become the guidepost of our experiences.

"During the first 7-10 years of our lives, our subconscious mind works like a video recorder. It simply records all the external events in our lives, and then it begins associating feelings, memories, and beliefs with those events. As we grow older, we begin to form subconscious beliefs about everything we come into contact with. As we form these beliefs we then begin making assumptions about who we are and how we fit into the world. Our prerecorded tapes become our subconscious beliefs about ourselves, and everything we think and do are then filtered through, and influenced by, these prerecorded tapes."

Without question, our minds are very powerful tools that can be used to create or destroy our lives. It's important that we recognize just how powerful our mind truly is. To fully understand our minds, we must first begin by acknowledging that there is a power greater than ourselves in the universe that we have direct access to. This power has nothing to do with organized religion or religious dogma and doctrine, although most people do learn about this power through religion. You can call this power whatever you choose, but it is important that you create a connection and intimacy with it. I believe our minds are the direct link to this divine power and when we access it, nothing is impossible.

Remember this quote by Dr. Wayne Dyer: *"What you think about expands. If your thoughts are centered on what you're not getting in your life, then what you're not getting, by definition, will have to expand."*

There are some philosophers who believe that our thoughts

create our reality and if this is true (which I believe it is), this means that we can use our minds to create anything we want. This points to the quote by Napoleon Hill that states: *"Whatever the mind of man can conceive and believe you can achieve."*

Which leads us to the origin of stereotypes. Remember my definition of stereotype? *"A stereotype is an unconscious, subconscious belief that we hold in our minds about a person or a thing."* If we believe something about a person or thing in our minds, then that is how they show up in our reality.

Let me explain what I mean.

Try to imagine a person who happens to be white. This person has no experience dealing with black people. They have no black friends, their parents have no black friends, they go to an all-white school and they were raised in an all-white neighborhood.

Since they have no direct experience with black people, where/how did they form their beliefs (stereotypes) about black people?

Using the analogy that our minds work like a video recorder, we must recognize that our beliefs/stereotypes come from three primary sources:

1. **Our Families**
2. **Our Culture**
3. **Our Media**

The primary source of our beliefs and stereotypes originate

from our parents. In this case, let's imagine that the white person's parents happened to be racist. So the child grows up and records everything they hear their parents say about people of other races. They begin creating a subconscious belief/stereotype that says *black people are inferior and different*. As the child grows up, they also hear some of the same sentiments from people in their neighborhoods and other social circles. Now they are being influenced by their culture. Their culture can include their social circles, churches, organizations, and even social media. In most cases, their cultural influences will be from people who also happen to be white.

Last but definitely not least, the media generates the majority of beliefs/stereotypes. Although our families are the primary source of our initial beliefs about ourselves, I believe the media has a more profound impact on our beliefs about the world around us.

Going back to our example, if the white person tunes into the media about black people, they will be bombarded with negative images and stereotypes. Therefore, their subconscious programming about black people will be negative.

So what happens when this white person meets a black person for the very first time? Since they have no personal experience with black people, their automatic response is to access their beliefs about black people, which are stored in their subconscious minds.

Remember what I said about the subconscious mind being

1000% more powerful than the conscious mind? This is where stereotypes become activated. No matter what the white person may think about their initial contact with the black person (they may appear nice and trustworthy), their subconscious mind will overrule their conscious mind and the negative beliefs will surface. They may have thoughts like: *I don't trust them; maybe they will try to rob me; I better be careful around them.* All of these thoughts are driven by subconscious beliefs. Unfortunately, the white person isn't even aware that their thoughts are being driven by their subconscious mind.

Of course, this is a simplified explanation of how the mind works, but rest assured this *is* how it works. The story I used above was just to make a point. The story could easily be reversed and the white person could have grown up in an environment in which their programming about black people was positive. Or, it could have been a story about a black person whose programming was negative about white people. The point is, a stereotype *is an unconscious, subconscious belief that we hold in our minds about a person or a thing.*

Here is another way to look at it. Here is an excerpt from my very first book titled *Brothers Are You Listening?* (Creation Publishing Group LLC published in 1995).

Let's take a moment and think about the power of belief. Remember when you were a kid and you believed in Santa Claus, or maybe the Easter Bunny? Maybe you won't admit to that, but how about when you believed in monsters?

Remember sitting up thinking that there was a monster in

your closet, and you were scared to death? Although these things weren't real, our belief in them created fear, happiness, sadness, and excitement. As children, we were extremely open-minded and it was easy for us to believe almost anything. As we become older, we become a little more skeptical and not as gullible, and it's almost impossible to get us to believe anything we can't prove or quantify.

The point is that as long as it's real in our minds, then our bodies respond with appropriate actions and reactions. Here's another example. Imagine that you are out of town and you get a call and someone says that your mom has died. If you believe it then you will more than likely experience pain and sorrow. You may become sad and begin to cry, or you may simply become depressed. So what if you went home and found out that it wasn't true? Imagine that it was a case of mistaken identity and your mom was fine, now what would you experience? Happiness, joy, whatever. The point is, at the time you believed your mom was dead your entire being shifted into a response that was appropriate to your feelings and belief about death. Your belief in her death created the experience of death within your mind. I'm not going to try to explain the entire process, I simply want to give you a foundation to build on.

Our beliefs about ourselves and the world around us have a lot to do with the experiences we create in our lives. If you've ever studied the great spiritual masters you will find that most of their teachings were based on belief or faith. It's been defined as *"evidence of things unseen."* It is the beliefs that we hold in our minds that create the world around us. There is a metaphysical saying, *"Thoughts held in mind create likes of its kind."* There is definitely a lot of validity to that statement.

Another perfect analogy of how this process works is the personal computer. When a computer is first assembled there is absolutely no information in it. It's basically an empty box of wires, circuits, and chips. Once you decide what you want your computer to do, you have the option to add different programs. You can also install memory and other items, but since I'm making a simple analogy I won't bore you with technicalities. The point that I want to make is the computer has a device called a hard drive. The hard drive is located within the body of the computer and in most cases, it will not be removed. It stores your main programs on what's called a hard disk. The information that is stored on this hard disk is semi-permanent. As I mentioned, once you purchase your computer, you have the option as to what information you want to program on that hard disk.

In addition to the hard disk the computer can accept information from CD, which contains information that can be fed into the computer externally. It contains information that you insert into the computer, and the computer takes that information, then processes it and responds.

I want you to remember that the hard disk is the internal disk and the CD is the external disk. I will be referring back to this analogy.

So let's use an example of how this process works. Let's imagine that we have two children born at the same time in the same hospital. When these babies are born their minds are basically blank (just like the new computer). Baby #1 comes into a family that is nurturing and loving. When the parents take her home, they are constantly cuddling her and providing her with love and affection. They tell baby #1 how beautiful she is and how happy they are that she was born. They give her positive affirmations and shower her with compliments.

Baby #2, on the other hand, has parents that are constantly telling her how stupid she is. All she hears is how her parents wish she had never been born. She is constantly yelled at and neglected. They also tell her how ugly she is.

What is actually taking place the first three years of these children's lives is that their parents are loading their hard disk with information or beliefs about themselves. This information becomes semi-permanent on that child's hard disk. This information will be the foundation for how that child feels about themselves for the rest of their lives, or until that child decides to change that information. It is the basis for a person's self-esteem.

So, based on this scenario, what type of beliefs do you think each child will have about itself?

Now that we know what type of information is stored on their hard disk, let's talk about inserting some information on a CD.

Let's imagine that information was "I really think you're beautiful." Now, remember, we're putting in information from an external disk. When we do that, the computer has to take that external information, then process it before it can respond. If the computer has the same information stored on the hard disk it can process it, then respond in the appropriate manner. If it doesn't have that information, it will reject the outside information.

When baby #1 receives the information, she takes it, processes it, finds that information on her hard disk, then responds with an accepting *"Thank you."* On the other hand, baby #2 receives the information but when she tries to process it, her mind can't find it on her hard drive. So she rejects that information and responds with something like *"No you don't!"* and turns away.

No matter how hard you try, you cannot get baby #2 to accept that information. What has happened is baby #2 has created a belief that no one loves her. And because of this belief, she will never be able to accept love from anyone unless she goes in and erases the negative beliefs from her hard drive and replaces them with positive beliefs.

Take a moment and think about your childhood. Ask yourself - what are some of the beliefs you created about yourself that may need to be changed? As simplistic as it sounds, that's exactly the way our minds work. We form beliefs based on the information we have stored on our hard disk. The first few years of life are the most critical. That's when we are programming our minds.

As I mentioned, the information that is stored on our hard disk is semi-permanent. That means it can be changed. But it takes a willing participant with a commitment to himself or herself to make the changes. This process can be emotionally painful. But it is my belief that there are no shortcuts. If you really want to replace the old beliefs with new beliefs, you have to be willing to start at the beginning. That means identifying the origin of the beliefs and being able to erase all the old information and replace it with new information.

Stereotypes are simply learned unconscious beliefs. The good news is that stereotypes can be changed. Since stereotypes are learned, they can be *un*learned, and that is the intention of this book. If you have negative stereotypes about black men, I want you to be open to changing them to positive. To do so, you must be willing to discover any unwarranted negative stereotypes you may be holding on to and be willing to accept some more positive ones.

To shed further light on stereotypes and where they come from, I want to share a conversation I had with a friend of mine. It was actually more of a heated discussion about whether or not America was a racist country.

The discussion went something like this.

Friend: "America is such a racist country. A black man doesn't stand a chance in this country. Just look at what they do to black men. Police kill black men and get away with murder. The current president is a racist and most white people agree with him and his racist views."

Me: "So you think the entire country is racist?"

Friend: "The majority of them are. Don't you watch the news?"

Me: "So let me get clear on what you mean. You believe that this country is so racist that it can keep black men from succeeding?"

Friend: "Absolutely! The system is rigged against black men. They control everything and it's almost impossible for black men to get ahead."

Me: "So who are they? Who specifically are the men that are holding black men back?"

Friend: "The white men who control the government and the corporations. They are the ones who control the country. They are the ones who control the media. They are the ones who control the judicial system."

Me: "So you believe that there are actually groups of men who are intentionally trying to keep black men down? You believe there is a conspiracy against black men and this group of white men is controlling us?

Friend: "Absolutely!"

Me: "I must admit that I completely disagree with your beliefs. I refuse to believe that there is a group of men who are intentionally working to keep black men down. I don't see how that is possible. I don't believe anyone can stop me from accomplishing anything I set my mind to. I recognize that we have lots of challenges as black men but I believe your assertion that there is a group of white men specifically trying to hold us back perpetuates a mindset of victimization and it doesn't help black men at all. It implies that we are powerless and not in control of our own destinies and I definitely disagree with that."

Friend: "That's because you're one of those unrealistic optimistic people. You guys don't live in the real world. You're in denial and can't even see the problems that are right there in front of you. America is a racist country."

Me: "I respect your beliefs and definitely care about you as a friend. Although we have different points of view it doesn't change how I feel about you. Yes, I am an optimist and will continue to be one and I would hope that you would at least be open to the possibility that you're wrong about this country."

~~~~~~~~~~~~~

Needless to say, my friend had some pretty negative stereotypes about America and about white people. It was not my place to judge him for his views because I recognized that his views didn't actually define him. He was and still is, a very good friend of mine. We simply have different viewpoints and mindsets.

~~~~~~~~~~~~~

After our conversation, I spent a lot of time processing what my friend said. I realized that there are a lot of people who think and believe the same things my friend believes, and it is my intention to try to change the minds and hearts of people who do.

I have come to know that the key to changing a lot of the problems facing our world is to simply change our beliefs. It may sound oversimplified, but I am absolutely convinced that our thoughts and beliefs really do create our reality, and if we want to change our outer world we must begin by changing our *inner* world first.

With that being said, I wanted to share my thoughts about what my friend said about America being a racist country. It is my fervent belief that without question America is not a racist country. Are there racists that inhabit the US? Of course! The problem as I see it is we tend to refer to America as though it were a person. When people talk about the atrocities of slavery and discrimination they refer to America as though it were a single person that was acting out on its own and causing these things to happen. We must accept the truth that America is comprised of a diverse group of people who make up this great country. So America is simply a reflection of the consciousness of the people who live here. Since the majority of people living in the US, for the most part, have been white people (except when they first invaded America), this country has what I call a *Collective White Belief System* (CWBS). The CWBS has controlled this country for a very long time, but as the country has become more diverse, the CWBS is losing its influence and power.

When people talk about institutionalized racism and white privilege, what they are speaking of is the CWBS. It is a belief system based on white superiority that goes back hundreds of years. Another reason for my optimism is the fact that each generation moves further and further away from the CWBS. During the '60s and the Civil Rights Movement, the CWBS began shifting. The pioneers of the civil rights movement convinced enough white people that segregation and the treatment of people of color were wrong. This was no easy task. Changing the CWBS wasn't easy. That's why there was lunch counter sit-ins. That's why there was a march on Washington. That's why Dr. King's dream speech was so important. In order to shift the CWBS, a tipping point had to be reached, and once it did things began to change.

So, what is the tipping point? There are some people who believe that once 51 percent of the population agrees on a new belief then that belief changes the collective consciousness of the country. Using the example of the Civil Rights Movement, once 51 percent of white people changed their minds then the CWBS changed, and the civil rights movement was accepted and it changed the country.

Despite the apparent racial conflict that is still going on in this country, I believe that the CWBS is still being broken down and this country can achieve racial harmony. As a matter of fact, I believe it's inevitable. There is always chaos before creation, and the current racial chaos we're experiencing will eventually lead to unity. You may be asking why I believe this and you may believe that I am a pie-in-the-sky-dreamer, but it is my belief that there is divine order in the Universe and that power that is greater than myself is orchestrating the entire cosmos. This Divine Intelligence has an intention, and that is to create heaven right here on earth and nothing can thwart that intention.

This does not mean that the CWBS does not exist. Quite the contrary. It still exists, and it still influences the minds and hearts of a lot of people in this country. Proof of this can be found in our current president. It can also be found in the racially motivated attacks on people of color. It can be found when white police officers kill black men and are acquitted of any crime, despite irrefutable evidence. It can be found in the disproportionate coverage of negative stories about black men. It is alive and well in this country, but as mentioned, I see a light at the end of the tunnel and I am absolutely certain that the CWBS can be changed to the Collective Universal Belief System in which all human beings are accepted for who they are and their diversity is celebrated.

It's been said that the first step in solving a problem is admitting you have one. To get rid of the CWBS, we must be willing to admit that it exists. Since the media contributes so much to our beliefs and perpetuates so many stereotypes, it's important for us to acknowledge that the majority of people that control our media happen to be white. They are driven by the CWBS, and although they may not be intentionally trying to hurt black people or hold them back, the result is still the same. They are contributing to the negative stereotypes of black men. So rather than call them racists, I will assert that they are biased based on the CWBS. In order for them to change that bias, we must continue to bring it to their attention by speaking out against the unequal coverage of black men and violence and to challenge them to showcase the positive stories as equally as they do the negative ones.

But even more importantly, we must ensure that we are sharing our own positive stories with the world. Just like the CWBS exists, so too does the Collective Black Belief System. Unfortunately, the CBBS can be even more destructive than the CWBS.

The reason this is true is because in a lot of cases the CBBS is attacking the CWBS for its unfair portrayal of black people, and yet at the same time our media is filled with as much negativity as the white media. The constant barrage and attack of the CWBS perpetuate the idea that "all" white people and institutions are working against black people, and it creates feelings of powerlessness and victimization. The CWBS promotes an *"us versus them"* belief system, which creates anger, frustration, and division.

The one thing the CWBS refuses to acknowledge is the fact that, collectively speaking, America loves violence. This is evidenced by the movies we watch, the music we listen to, the books and magazines we read, and of course the news that we watch. Just take a moment and think about the successful movies, music, and magazines in America. The majority of them are overwhelmingly violent and negative. Companies create products and services based on demand; if the demand wasn't there, they would stop creating the content. So who are the people who are demanding this type of content? Since black people only make up approximately 13% of America, you can rest assured that we aren't responsible for this obsession with violence. The violence is driven by the CWBS, simply because they are the majority of people who are demanding this content.

Since the CWBS thrives on violence and negativity, the key to our success lies in our ability and willingness to disengage from the CWBS and make sure we are not contributing to the violence and negativity ourselves. We must be willing to move past the negative media-generated stereotypes and provide ourselves with the resources that help us overcome the multiplicity of challenges we are faced with to start building a brighter future for humanity as a whole.

My hope is that this chapter has challenged you to think and has shed some light on where stereotypes come from, and how we can change them.

It all begins with you.

Are you willing to look at the negative stereotypes you may have about black men?

Are you willing to engage in a dialog that encourages black men to reach their full potential?

The following chapters about the 10 most destructive media-generated illusions about black men are going to shed some light on how the CWBS contributes to the negative stereotypes about black men. It's important that you contemplate these illusions and make sure that you do not act consistently with any of them. I can assure you that if you wake up from these illusions and take 100% responsibility for your life, there is nothing you cannot be, do, or have. But you must begin by changing your inner mindset, and then I promise you that your outer reality will change to match it.

I'd like to leave you with a quote from Muhammad Ali:

> *"It's the repetition of affirmations that leads to belief. And once that belief becomes a deep conviction, things begin to happen."*

This quote is a double-edged sword. Your affirmations can be positive or negative. As soon as you commit to either one, those beliefs will determine your destiny.

My recommendation is that you choose to focus on positive affirmations, which will create positive beliefs, leading to positive actions and will create positive outcomes.

Good luck!

"We are not fighting for integration, nor are we fighting for separation. We are fighting for **recognition as human beings***...In fact, we are actually fighting for rights that are even greater than civil rights and that is human rights."*

- Malcolm X
Black Revolution

Illusion #1

Black Men Are an Endangered Species

In 1995, I overheard a conversation between two apparently well-educated, well-dressed, and professional young black men. They were having a conversation about the eradication of black men from America. They were both convinced that all black men would be extinct within twenty years.

It was heartbreaking to listen to their conversation, so I decided to ask them if they really believed what they were saying. As I approached them, I could sense their feelings of hopelessness. Their conversation and demeanor suggested that they had given up hope for the future and felt completely victimized by a society that, in their view, was trying to do everything in its power to keep them from succeeding.

I walked over to their table and apologized for eavesdropping on their conversation. I then asked them if they truly believed what they were saying about black men being eradicated within a twenty-year time frame. One of the young men looked me dead in the eyes and said: "Absolutely. I truly believe that black men will be extinct in twenty years. Don't you watch the news? In twenty years all black men will either be dead or in prison."

As I looked into his eyes I could sense his strong conviction that the future was bleak for black men. In his mind, black men were an endangered species and there was nothing anyone could do about it. I knew there was nothing I could have said that would change his mind, so I simply looked at him with a smile, put my hand on his shoulder, and said:

"Don't believe the hype my brother, don't believe the hype. Never trust the media to tell you the truth about black men. We are actually doing a lot better than most people think. Keep your head up! The future is bright if you choose to believe that it can be."

He looked at me with confusion and disbelief in his eyes and didn't say a word. I then walked away feeling a little sad and a little inspired at the same time. I felt sad that they really believed there was a black male crisis that would lead to our eradication. But most importantly I felt inspired because that conversation challenged me.

Immediately after that conversation, I made a commitment that I was going to do something to change the mindset of black men in America. I instinctively knew that the conversation the men were having was a microcosm of how too many black men feel. There are too many who believe that America is doing everything in its power to eradicate us, and they feel powerless and victimized.

But what could I do? Who was I to believe that I could actually do something to help? How could I help black men change their mindset and give them reasons for optimism? I didn't have any resources or education, and I didn't know what I was going to do, but I simply just intuitively knew that I could and would do something.

During this time, I had been involved with my own journey of transformation. I had been working with a therapist and began my journey of healing and recovering from some major trauma from my childhood. I read books on human potential, psychology, personal growth, and spirituality. I attended lectures and listened to audio-tapes that helped me overcome some major depression, and I was now on the road to becoming truly happy with myself.

After a few months, I realized what I needed to do in response to the conversation I had had with the men at the restaurant. In order for me to do something to support black men in overcoming a negative mindset, I needed to write a book to share my journey of healing!

At the time I knew absolutely nothing about writing a book. This was before the Internet was popular and I had no idea where to begin, so I decided to do some research and learn everything I could about writing a book. I went to the library and researched and after a few weeks, I had enough information to begin. The first thing I had to do was decide what I wanted to write about. I kept thinking about the conversation I had in the restaurant and I asked myself what I would say to them through this book. As I thought about our brief conversation, a title just popped into my mind: ***Brothers***

Are You Listening? The title was perfect! Since the purpose of the book was to share my personal journey of transformation, the question I asked myself was whether or not black men would listen to my message. I had a lot of fear about sharing my journey, but based on how much I had grown and changed my own life, I really believed that my message could help change other people's lives too. *Brothers Are You Listening?* captured the essence of the message I wanted to share.

After a few months, I completed the book and was then faced with another set of challenges: how was I going to get it published? I went back to the library and did more research about publishers. I learned that in order to get a publisher interested in your work you had to pitch to them, so I submitted my query letter to more than 50 different publishers and received 50 different rejections.

But that didn't stop me. I was committed to getting my message out there and no matter what it took I was going to get my book published. I then had a bright idea. Since I wanted to learn about book publishing, why not get a job at a bookstore? Brilliant idea! I was able to secure a part-time job at a bookstore and I became a sponge for information about book publishing. The best part of the job was being able to take home any book I wanted to read without having to buy it. I learned everything I could about the publishing world, and that is when I decided that I wanted to start my own publishing company.

Fast forward approximately 23 years, and I've written and

published six books, including this one, and I already have titles, book covers, and chapter outlines for six more. My commitment is to write one book per year as I build my publishing company to eventually help others publish their books. I simply love writing books!

Without question, I've made a positive impact on the lives of hundreds of men around the globe. What began as a simple idea to help black men change their mindset has now evolved into a publishing company that empowers all men, regardless of race, to embrace a new paradigm of masculinity which I believe can help remove the majority of social ills facing our world today.

I wanted to share that brief story in the hopes that you get a sense that nothing is impossible if you want it badly enough. I am a living example and proof that you can live your dreams if you're willing to put forth the effort. But I want to get back to the purpose of this chapter. I want you to realize that black men are not an endangered species, and despite what you may have seen through the media, we are actually in a position to experience unprecedented levels of success in America.

So, let's talk about why so many people have actually accepted the illusion that we are endangered. If you pay attention to our media, it should be easy to see why so many people have accepted this illusion. When we see stories of black men being killed by police, it provides evidence to some people that we are being eradicated. The constant barrage of negative imagery creates the belief system and stereotype in our minds that **all** white police officers intentionally set out to kill black men.

So, let me be clear about this point: it is an absolute travesty of justice to see a black man being killed by police. In no way do I want to minimize the impact of what seeing a black man being killed by a police officer has on the psyche of black men. My heart is still broken by the violent murder of Philando Castille, Michael Brown, Eric Garner, Alton Sterling, Trayvon Martin, and Tavir Rice, to just name a few. I understand how painful and terrorizing it can be just thinking about the possibility that a black man will be killed by someone who is sworn to protect and serve. Even more devastating is how the police officers who actually commit these crimes are not held responsible for their deaths, and in most cases are not even reprimanded for their actions - this is the real tragedy!

But the point I'm making here is to share a few facts about black male deaths by police officers. Since my intention is to shatter the illusion that black men are an endangered species, let's take a look at some verifiable statistics from the FBI database from 2015:

- There were **8,248,709** arrests made in 2015, and per the Washington Post database, there were **991** fatal police altercations with suspects. This makes the probability of **anyone** being fatally shot when arrested by a police officer **1 in 8,323**.

- The number of **blacks killed by police** was **258**. The number of black people who were arrested totaled **2,197,140**. This puts the probability of an **arrested black**

person being killed by a police officer at **1 in 8,516**.

- **5,753,212** white people were arrested and **495** killed by police officers, so **1 in 11,622**.

What this means is that because the probability is so low — roughly 0.01 percent in each case — it is virtually nonexistent for anyone to be killed while being arrested.

The evidence here speaks for itself. The reality is, the chances of a black male being killed by a police officer is extremely low. Once again, I do not want to excuse the obvious violence against black men, but we cannot hold on to the stereotype and belief that black men are being eradicated by police officers.

Another reason some people subscribe to the notion that black men are an endangered species is because of high incarceration rates. But if we look closely enough, we should be able to see that although the incarceration rate may be high there should be no cause for concern that all black men are going to end up in jail as the men in the restaurant believed.

According to Keith Humphreys, who is a Professor of Psychiatry at Stanford University and is an affiliated faculty member at Stanford Law School and the Stanford Neurosciences Institute (and also happens to be white):

"There's been a big decline in the black incarceration rate, and almost nobody's paying attention."

He writes in the Washington Post, February 10, 2016:

"After decades of growth, the U.S. imprisonment rate has

been declining for the past six years. Hidden within this welcome overall trend is a sizable and surprising racial disparity: African-Americans are benefitting from the national de-incarceration trend but whites are serving time at increasingly higher rates.

*"The pattern of results, evident in a series of reports from the Bureau of Justice Statistics, is most stark among women. Since 2000, the imprisonment rate among African-American women has dropped 47 percent, while the rate among white women has risen by 56 percent. These trends have combined to shrink the racial disparity in women's imprisonment by two-thirds. A similar pattern emerges for men, who compose a much larger share of the prison population. **The rate of imprisonment among African-American men remains very high, but nonetheless, it has tumbled 22 percent since 2000.** The rate for white men, in contrast, is 4 percent higher than it was in 2000. As a result, the racial disparity has shrunk by nearly one quarter.*

"In responding to the data, Fordham University Professor John Pfaff echoed several criminologists when he said that "This is one of the most surprising pattern of results I have seen in corrections in a long time." Pfaff said that "law enforcement attitudes getting tougher in rural areas and softer in urban areas may be contributing to this change."

Adam Gelb, who directs the public safety performance project of the Pew Charitable Trusts, suggested that: *"changes in drug use and enforcement over the past 15 years could be at play."* Gelb said the methamphetamine, prescription opioid, and heroin epidemics, have affected whites more so than the crack cocaine epidemic, which increased incarceration among blacks in the 1980s and 1990s but has since waned.

Stanford Law School Professor Joan Petersilia noted another possible cause: *"sex offenders, who are disproportionately white and tend to receive long sentences, are a new target for the war on crime."* Consistent with this explanation, a larger proportion of white inmates have been convicted of sex crimes (16.4 percent) than have black inmates (8 percent).

More generally, multiple indicators of health and well-being have shown evidence of deterioration in white Americans over the past 15 years, including rising rates of suicide, drug overdose, poor mental health, and inability to work.

Whatever cultural and macroeconomic forces are producing these changes, these could also conceivably be driving increased involvement in the criminal justice system by whites, including rising imprisonment in an era of de-incarceration.

~~~~~~~~~~~~

My point once again, is that the media has perpetuated the idea that black men are continuously being incarcerated at an alarming rate and therefore are destined for eradication. Evidence of this can be found in a comment made by former presidential candidate Bernie Sanders (who I actually endorsed and still have the utmost respect for). In an interview with Charlie Rose on June 11, 2015, he stated: *"A black male baby born today, if we do not change the system, stands a 1 in 3 chance ending up in jail. This is an unspeakable tragedy."*

It turns out that his statistic was from a report written in 2001 by the Bureau of Justice Statistics, and they had not been updated to reflect the current trends which showed that the incarceration rates for black men had actually **declined** by approximately 20% in 10 years, which would definitely change the percentages more positively. But once he made the comment the media jumped on the story, and pretty soon there were media headlines everywhere stating that **1 in 3 black men will end up in jail in their lifetime.**

This is how the Collective White Belief System works. Though it may be unintentional, once a story like this gets into the media, it becomes a stereotype difficult to change. A lot of white people then accept it as truth when in reality it isn't. At the same time, black people accept it as truth and use it as evidence that we are an endangered species.

The last source of eradication that the young men in the restaurant were talking about was murder. The fact is that the **number one** cause of death for black males between the ages of 18 and 35 is homicide. This is not a stereotype, it is a documented fact. Of course, this creates an endless supply of media stories too, about black-on-black crime and the eradication of black males. Politicians use it to get votes, news outlets use it to get viewership, and even black organizations use it to secure funding. This is a reality and something that **must** be addressed head-on. But should we be afraid that this will lead to the extinction of black men? I believe the answer is an emphatic **no**!

According to an article by US News and World Report dated Sept. 29, 2016, by Matthew Cella and Alan Neuhauser, there were 2,380 black men killed by other black men in 2015. Without question, this is a huge problem and one that must be addressed. But does it warrant the fear that all black men will eventually be eradicated? Of course, it doesn't. Once again, I am not discounting the tragedy of murder. My point here is that far too many of our young black men literally believe that we are being eradicated from society. We must do everything we can to change their mindset. Although there are challenges which must be addressed, there should be no fear that we are on the verge of extinction.

So, let's put this into context. According to the US Census Bureau, in 2013 there were 21.5 million black males in America. Approximately 2,500 black men that are killed per year. That means that 0.01 of black men are killed per year if the population and amount of murders stay the same. Based on this number alone, there should be no fear of black men being eradicated.

The problem as I see is the fact that the CWBS constantly tries to racialize violence and misconstrue it to make it appear that *violence* is a *black* problem. **The truth is that violence is violence, regardless of race.** White people and black people violently kill each other for the same reason, which is always driven by anger. The only way to remove the violence from our society is to recognize that anger is a human emotion that can be controlled. By giving men the tools to appropriately deal with their anger, we will see a decline in violent acts.

Of course, statistics can be construed to mean whatever you want them to mean, so let me share more of my beliefs about why I believe black men are not an endangered species.

Firstly, as more black people become attorneys, judges, politicians, and law officers, I believe we will continue to see a trend of decreased incarceration. The evidence is overwhelming regarding the unfair representation black males receive due to poverty and educational levels, and the more blacks we have serving in the judicial system the more likely we are to receive fair treatment. I also believe the CWBS is also changing and becoming more compassionate and understanding of the challenges facing black males, while there is also a movement to decrease the prison population in general. I also believe that each generation is less prejudiced and racist than the previous generation because of human evolution, which will lead to changes in the justice system and the media portrayal of black men moving forward.

Secondly, I believe the issue of police brutality has been brought front and center in this country and most people want to see changes in how police officers interact with men of color. There are no easy solutions to this issue, but the exposure that has been generated by Colin Kaepernick's refusal to stand for the national anthem to protest police brutality has created a movement to bring about changes in police behavior and hopefully to hold police accountable for their actions.

Thirdly, I believe movements like Black Lives Matter are

bringing awareness to the fact that we still have a way to go in terms of race relations, but young people are rallying together to make changes. As I watch people of all races supporting this movement (and of course, there are those who vehemently oppose it) and encouraging racial unity, it fills me with hope and optimism for the future.

And last, but definitely not least, I fervently believe that the overwhelming majority of white people in this country are not racists and they are interested in creating solutions to the multiplicity of challenges facing America. As human beings, we all want the same things: to love and be loved; to have access to the American dream; to be judged by the content of our character, not the color of our skin; to have meaning and purpose in our lives; and to make the world a little better in our own simple way.

So, if you've been holding on to the idea that black men are an endangered species, I invite you to let go of it right now and recognize that we are here to contribute to this country and to be an **asset** not a **liability**. We love America and we aren't going anywhere!

"Not everything that is faced can be changed; but nothing can be changed until it is faced."

- James Baldwin
As Much Truth As One Can Bear
New York Times

Illusion #2

Black Men Use Race as an Excuse for Failure

On August 14, 2017, a group of white nationalists and white supremacists held a *Unite the Right* rally in Charlottesville, Virginia, in protest of the removal of a Confederate statue. As I watched the protest on television, it was difficult to believe that this was actually occurring in 2017. It felt more like an event from 1960. Although it was a shocking sight, nothing was more shocking to me than the current president of the United States indirectly supporting the march and the neo-Nazi protesters. His refusal to denounce the actions of the white supremacy group spoke volumes about where he stands in regard to race relations. My first thought was *how can the president of the United States not condemn the actions of neo-Nazis?* Isn't it the job of the president to bring the country together?

As the media went into a frenzy, I ran across a social media post by a white guy who was trying to make sense of the events. He wanted to know what could be done to help the country come together, to remove the anger and hatred and replace it with unity and love.

In his post, he asked if people would simply share their feelings about the event without attacking or criticizing other people's opinions. I believed he was very sincere in his request, so I decided to write a response to his post:

> As a man who happens to be black, I resonate with your intention of this post Michael. I have personally been attacked by members of the KKK (not physically but through threatening letters, defacing my property and verbal threats, and abuse), and I have every reason to be appalled, angry, and offended by the events in Charlottesville. However, I do not feel any of those things. I mostly feel sad. I am saddened by the unnecessary violence, the loss of life, the racial division, and the impact this is having on our youth.
>
> I'm saddened because there is so much healing needed for men who are acting out of their own hurt and unconsciousness, and yet they are too proud or too afraid to look at their own inner wounding that is driving their behavior. I'm sad because I recognize that there are actually solutions to this hatred and anger that will never be found through political, educational, or even religious means. It saddens me to say this because most people will assume that I'm condoning the hatred and violence by saying that only a hurt person hurts another person and I know that I will be called a sellout by people of color because I do not share the anger and rage that so many of them feel.
>
> My belief that having empathy and compassion for those who attempt to hurt us causes a tug of war in my mind

and heart. On one hand I know love is the only thing that can change this situation, and on the other hand it feels as if I should be angry about the actions of the racists. But I don't. I feel absolutely no anger. Frustration is as close as I can get to anger right now. Frustrated that so many men are caught up in their wounding and have no idea that it is possible for them to release it and be free. Frustrated in knowing that my work can help men heal, yet realizing few men are willing to accept the support.

And yet I remain optimistic. I'm optimistic because I'm aware that there are lots of men who are now doing their work. I'm optimistic because you had the courage to even post this into this feed. I'm optimistic because I have men of all ethnicities that read my books about redefining masculinity, listen to my podcast about a new conversation with men, and are close intimate friends with whom I would trust with my life.

So, despite the tragedy, I still see a light at the end of the tunnel. I see this light because I believe in a Divine Intelligence that created this amazing Universe and I believe that its ultimate intention is to create heaven on Earth and my job is to work hand-in-hand with it to ensure that it happens.

So, I do my work, share my gifts, and do my part in making the world a better place. That is all that is required of me.

~~~~~~~~~~~~~~

There are some people who believe we live in a post-racial America, which makes no sense to me because if it were truly *post-racial* we wouldn't be having a conversation about race. The truth is, race **does** matter, and we still have some ways to go in terms of race relations. This being said, I do not believe that race relations are actually getting worse in this country. Despite the apparent challenges we have in regard to race, I remain optimistic that race relations can and will improve in the immediate future. There is a stereotype that says all black men use race as an excuse for failure, and I want you to dispel that stereotype **right now**. If you aren't a black male it will be difficult, if not impossible, for you to empathize or understand the challenges of being a black man in America. This isn't using race as an excuse - it's an undeniable fact.

There's a scene in the movie *Crash* in which Terrence Howard plays a successful black man in Hollywood who is driving home one night when he and his wife are pulled over by a racist police officer. The police officer assaults him and his wife, and there is nothing he can do about it. In the scene, he is absolutely powerless. If he resists, there is the possibility he will be arrested, or even worse, killed. By not being able to say anything or to defend himself, he begins to feel inadequate in protecting himself and his wife. So, what should he do? Should he attempt to save his wife from the assault of the police officer? Should he resist the officer's attack and risk becoming just another statistic of a black male senselessly killed by a racist cop?

He decides to cooperate with the police officer and eventually the police officer lets him go. As he is driving home, there is silence between him and his wife. He obviously feels emasculated and humiliated as a man. You can feel the anger inside of him and there is no outlet for him to release it. When they arrive home, his wife attacks him for not protecting her and blames him for the entire incident. She accuses him of not being a *real man* and completely invalidates his experience, unwilling to acknowledge the difficult choice he had to make in not resisting arrest. This scene is the perfect metaphor for being a black man in America.

I'm sure most black men can relate to the feeling of powerlessness that the character felt in that scene. Not only do we have to deal with outside forces like police officers or neo-Nazis marching, we also have to deal with inside forces that come from the people we care about who sometimes aren't supportive and understanding of the challenges we face.

As a man who happens to be black, I have found that the key to being successful here in America is to embrace a simple paradox. If I say there are unequal opportunities for black men in America because of racism, discrimination, and prejudice, then it becomes a true statement. If I also say there are unlimited opportunities for black men in America, that too becomes a true statement.

But how can that be? If racism and discrimination are real then how can there be unlimited opportunities for black men? Herein lies the paradox. It sounds like contradictory statements, yet they are both true.

I'd like to share a brief story from my own life to make my point.

When I was 18 years old, I secured a job with a company called *McCoy's Building Supply*. Although I was a high school dropout, I convinced the manager that if he gave me a chance I would become one of his best employees. His name was Dan and he believed in me and decided to give me a chance.

From the very beginning, I loved the job. I loved working with customers and had a real knack for customer service. Although I had no experience, Dan was willing to teach me everything he could about the building supply industry. I became a sponge for knowledge. I learned everything I could while working at the store and by reading books on my days off.

After a few months, Dan called me into his office and acknowledged me for the great job I was doing, wanting to know if I would be interested in joining their manager trainee program. Of course, the answer was yes, and I knew that I had found a career that would pay handsomely and help me reach some of my professional goals.

After our meeting, I immediately went home to tell my mom the good news. She was extremely proud and happy for me, but at the same time, she was extremely skeptical. She didn't believe that the company was going to allow me to become a manager and make the kind of money they were promising without me first gaining a college degree. I assured her that they would, and I was absolutely certain that I could climb the corporate ladder and eventually become manager of my own store.

A few months passed and I was doing extremely well. Although I wasn't officially an assistant manager yet Dan had given me lots of responsibilities and he was definitely preparing for me to move up the ladder.

A few more months passed and I learned that the owner of the store was coming to visit and I would have a chance to meet him. Dan told me to make sure I was on my best behavior, because if I impressed him it would definitely increase my chances of becoming a manager one day.

The day the owner was scheduled to come I had a picture in my mind of what he might look like: a JR. Ewing from the television show *Dallas*. When he walked into the store I was completely shocked! He was approximately 5' 7" and maybe weighed 130 pounds soaking wet. He had on a simple white button-down shirt and a cowboy bolo-type necklace, with high water blue jeans and cowboy boots. I actually started laughing when I first saw him. It was my first time meeting a multimillionaire and he definitely didn't look anything like I imagined.

Dan introduced me to him and I gave him a firm handshake and a big smile. He told me he had heard good things about me and he was glad I was working for the company. After his review of the store with Dan he asked me if there was anything else I would like to discuss before he left.

I told him about my conversation with my mom and how she was skeptical about me becoming a manager with his company. I told him that she didn't think I could become a manager because I didn't have a college degree and because I was black. He looked at me with a smile and reassured me that being black and not having a college degree would have no impact on my ability to become a manager. He told me that most of his managers didn't have college degrees. Their training program was designed to be hands-on, and they always hired from within the company, so there were actually no advantages to having a degree. And in regard to being black, he mentioned there had only been one black manager in the history of the company, and he was really hoping that I would become the second one.

As he spoke, I could hear the sincerity in his words. I knew he was telling the truth, and I had no doubt I would become a manager.

A few days later, he personally called my mom and assured her that I didn't need a college degree to become a manager. He told her what a great job I was doing with the company and how pleased he was to have me as an employee. He said that he was absolutely certain that one day I would be a manager.

At the time, it took approximately 4-5 years for a new employee to move up the ranks and become a manager. I did it in a little over three years. As a matter of fact, I actually became the youngest manager in the history of the company at the age of 22, and only the second black manager in the company's history.

Becoming a manager was one of the proudest accomplishments of my life. I'll never forget walking into the store on my first day with the keys, knowing that I was entirely responsible for running this multimillion-dollar company. The feeling was nondescript!

Of course, there were also lots of challenges.

The store I managed was in a small suburb called Pearland, just south of Houston, Texas. I didn't know it in the beginning, but it was just a few miles away from a city named Alvin that still had active KKK halls (it was 1983 at the time). The first challenge I faced was a couple of racist employees who definitely didn't like the fact that their manager was black. One guy in particular, who had a confederate flag tattoo, caused a lot of problems. Fortunately, I've never had a problem maintaining a professional attitude in a work environment, so I was able to appropriately deal with the problem and eventually fire him.

Another challenge was the customers. There were several customers who made it known that they weren't too happy with me being manager. They spray-painted racial epithets on my car, spoke racial slurs to my face, and one guy even threatened to hurt my family if I didn't leave. There was one incident when I asked to see a customer's driver's license as he was making a purchase and I was ringing him up. He handed me some sort of KKK ID card and had a huge smirk on his face. I took the card from him and held it up close to his face, telling him jokingly that it was a very good picture of him on his KKK card but I couldn't accept it as identification, and I needed to see his driver's license. The fact that I wasn't intimidated and joked with him seemed to really piss him off, but he complied and threw his license on the counter. To further provoke him, I told him that his KKK picture was better than his license picture. I wrote down his license number, handed it back, and told him to have a great day. As he walked away I think I saw smoke coming from his ears he was so angry.

The most confrontational experience I had as a manager occurred after being there for around a year. I was at the back of the store when I heard a customer screaming at one of my cashiers. I immediately walked over to him and asked what the problem was. He looked at me and I immediately knew he had a problem with me being black. He asked to speak to the manager and when I said I was actually the manager he said it couldn't be. He then said he wanted to speak to my boss. When I told him *I* was the boss, he looked at me straight in the eyes and screamed: "You can't be the boss because we don't allow niggers to run things here in Pearland. I want to speak to your boss! Tell him to come here right now!" I reassured him that there was no one above me at the store, but he refused to listen. He kept insisting that he wanted to speak to someone who was white and in charge.

I have to say, this guy was approximately 60-70 years old and pretty frail. In no way was I afraid of a physical confrontation because I could have snapped the poor guy in half. But I needed to de-escalate the situation, so I decided to ask him if he would like to speak to the owner of the store by phone. He agreed and I contacted the owner. I explained the situation to him and then handed the customer the phone. The customer then ranted about why he let a nigger run his store and asked why someone white couldn't help him with his problem. After listening to him vent for a while, I noticed the man's face change dramatically and he handed the phone back. He became quiet and I had no idea what the owner had said. The owner then told me to call the police to have him escorted out of the store and never allow him to come back.

Coincidently, a police officer happened to come in the store at the time and I explained what happened and that I needed him to escort the customer out. Now the guy was really angry, cursing and screaming and threatening me with physical violence. The police officer escorted him out and threatened to arrest him if he didn't calm down. The guy kept screaming and the police eventually arrested him and put him in the back of the police car. He asked me if I wanted to press any charges and after I said no he sat with the man to calm him down. Eventually, he did, so the police officer released him and the man drove away.

I never saw or heard from him again. After the confrontation, there were a few customers who came up to me and apologized for the man's behavior. One woman was almost in tears and she said how sorry she was for how the man acted. I told her not to worry and there was no need for an apology.

A few minutes after the man left, the owner called me back and asked how things were going. He thanked me for being so professional and not allowing the customer to get under my skin. He apologized for the man's actions and said he had no idea I had to deal with such racial hatred, but he said he was extremely proud of me for how I handled myself and he knew I was the perfect manager for that particular store. He had told the customer over the phone that I was the manager and I had the authority to make all decisions concerning the store. He then told him he didn't appreciate his derogatory comments, that he would not tolerate his behavior in his store, and that he was no longer welcome and needed to take his business elsewhere. Finally, he told the customer that he would be instructing me to contact the police to escort him out.

Once again, the owner thanked me for how I handled the situation and he acknowledged just how happy he was to have me as a manager.

After hanging up the phone, I felt a deep sense of pride. It felt great to have the unconditional support of my employer, and I knew I could count on him to support me in the future. But most importantly, I was proud of myself for how I handled the situation. I have dealt with racism and discrimination all my life and never allowed it to get in the way of achieving my goals.

I have never used race as an excuse for failure and I never will.

~~~~~~~~~~~~~

I share this story to point out that without question there are racist people in the world and it may not seem fair that we have to deal with it. It can sometimes seem as if the whole world is against us, simply because of the color of our skin. But we cannot allow anyone or anything to keep us from accomplishing our goals. It's easy to blame society, racism or racists for our failures in life. As I've shared in this story racism is real - but it can definitely be overcome.

I'm reminded of what Michelle Obama said when she stated: *"When they go low, we go high!"* These are words to live by.

Always go high!

So, if you ever hear a black man saying that it's difficult for them to make it in society and you aren't black before you judge him as playing the race card, take a moment and try to walk in his shoes. I'm not asking for your pity or sympathy, just a little compassion to recognize that there are certain challenges you don't have to deal with. Of course, there will be some black men that attempt to use race as an excuse no matter what you say, but they are few and far between, so don't group us all in that category.

If you're a man who happens to be black, simply commit to being the master of your destiny and never let racism or racists determine your fate.

You and you alone are responsible for your success, so grab fate by the horns and ride it into your destiny.

"It is the duty of the younger Negro artist...to change through the force of his art that old whispering 'I want to be white,' hidden in the aspirations of his people, to 'Why should I be white? I am a Negro—and beautiful!'"

- Langston Hughes
The Negro Artist and the Racial Mountain
The Nation

Illusion #3
Black Men Try To Be White

When I released my first book *Brothers Are You Listening?* back in 1995, I truly believed that black men would embrace my positive message. I was surprised when a few black men actually attacked me for writing the book. During one radio interview, a brother called in and accused me of trying to be white because I was talking about black men who were willing to go to therapy to get emotional support. His argument was that I had been reading books by *white men* who *didn't understand black culture* and therefore I was a sellout for not embracing African approaches and methodologies for dealing with racism.

Although there were a few men who felt that way, I think most black men were happy to hear a brother speaking so openly and authentically about emotional healing and personal development. I have since written three books specifically targeted to men of color, and I believe they are more open-minded than ever before and are definitely seeking more positive and inspirational resources to help them live extraordinary lives.

Amazingly, I still hear some black men say that I am attempting to be white, so I wanted to share an excerpt from *Brothers Are You Listening?* to reiterate my stance on being called a sellout.

This is an excerpt from the very first chapter: *The That's What White People Do Mentality.*

> If I had a nickel for every time I was accused of trying to be white, the money I would have accumulated by now would probably have exceeded the profits of this book. This is probably the hardest part about being a black male, in my opinion. This belief causes alienation and anger, and at times it seems like a no-win situation. As a race of people, we have to learn to accept our own diversity. As more and more of us assume positions of power, we have to learn to accept the fact that there is no longer a "black way of thinking." Because we choose to be open-minded does not mean we're selling out. We have to be able to base our decisions on our own beliefs and values and not conform to the way most people think we are supposed to think. Without question or hesitation, I can honestly say I have never even considered wanting to be white. As my grandfather taught me, I simply needed to think in the way of the man with all the money, not try to be like him. And that's exactly what I've done.
>
> All my life I've been attacked by my own people because I chose to speak properly and create the life I knew I deserved. This has to cease. We have to understand that we are individuals and we have the right and the

freedom to think and do anything we please. We have to be willing to accept our differences and still support each other.

We create a lot of separation amongst ourselves by our unwillingness to allow a black man to make decisions on his own. I believe we are paying a terrible price for these reactions. If we try to make our kids conform to a certain way of thinking how can we expect to move ahead? If our kids feel they have to conform, then we put limits on them and that is a shame. We must allow ourselves and our children to be open-minded and willing to take risks without the fear of expulsion from our race. Our future depends on it.

I have been fortunate in that I have always been exposed to people of other races. I learned very early that all people really are the same if you will take some time to get to know them. I have been blessed with a few white friends whom I would trust with my life, and I am truly grateful to have them in my life.

We must understand the importance of our diversity in this great country of ours. Some of you may have a lot of hatred and anger towards people of other races, but it is now time to lay our differences aside and create unity. It takes a real man to be the first to extend his hand in fellowship. I hope you will do just that.

I have a few questions I would like to ask you:

If a black man chooses to become a millionaire / billionaire, does that mean he's trying to be white?

If a black man chooses to participate in self-help seminars, does that mean he's trying to be white?

If a black man chooses to be affectionate in public with the woman he loves, does that mean he's trying to be white?

If a black man chooses to participate in his children's lives and doesn't believe in corporal punishment, does that mean he's trying to be white?

If a black man chooses to go bungee jumping, does that mean he's trying to be white?

If a black man chooses to be a Republican, does that mean he's trying to be white?

If a black man chooses to be monogamous, and love, cherish and adore his mate, does that mean he's trying to be white?

If a black man chooses to attend a majority white church because it really nurtures his soul, does that mean he's trying to be white?

The answer to each is an emphatic *No!* It simply means that he wants the best for himself and his family, and he deserves the best life has to offer.

We have to stop attacking each other because we choose to do something that is considered out of the norm. We have to accept the fact that the majority of white people in this country aren't racist and would gladly support us if we allowed them to. The time has come for us to not even have this color conversation. It's time to take control of our own destinies and create the life we deserve. We've "struggled" long enough. It's time to make a change and a new commitment to unity.

When you think of the Civil Rights Movement, what one word comes to mind? Freedom? Equality? Power? For me the one word is **access**. When I think of why our brothers and sisters gave their lives I realize that they simply wanted **access**. They knew that if they had **access** to the knowledge and information, then ultimately, they could achieve everything their white counterparts had achieved. So now that it's 2017, and we have that **access**, who's responsible for our success? **We are!**

It is completely up to us to take advantage of the doors that are wide open to us today. We must understand that our brothers and sisters died so that we could attend the workshops of our choice. They died so we could create close intimate relationships with our mates. They died so we could be better fathers and not subject our children to the pain they experienced. They died so we could base our political views on our own individual beliefs. They died so we could create strong family units that go on for generations. They died so we could bungee jump if that is our desire. And they died so that we could choose a God based on our soul's calling.

So, if we aren't taking full advantage of all the opportunities available to us right now, doesn't that mean that our brothers and sisters died in vain? To me that is absolutely unacceptable. I choose to take full advantage of every door that is open to me. That is the way that I repay my brothers and sisters of whom I am so very proud.

Ultimately as a Black American you only have two choices in which you can view our situation. First, you have the choice to view us as victims, a small group of people that is constantly abused, disrespected and on the edge of extinction. Or you can see us, as we truly are, a group of people that are the epitome of strength and perseverance; a group of people that know and live the word commitment. A group of people brought to a strange land with nothing but the clothes on their backs; brought to a place that was totally foreign and new. Because of their determination and courage, they were able to adapt, and despite seemingly insurmountable obstacles, they have prospered and cut their niche in a place that tried everything in their power to keep them separate.

How, my brothers, can you not be empowered by that? What other evidence do you need of our greatness? That, in itself, should be enough to inspire you to go out into the world with your head held high. So take a moment and acknowledge the greatness within you. You must understand that you are a very important part of history and no one is going to deny us what we deserve. Stand proud, my brothers, and bask in your greatness.

So my recommendation is that we, as black people, start supporting and empowering each other. We have to remove all these limiting beliefs and start working together. That means with people of all races. Yes, there are still a lot of ignorant people in the world and there are definitely challenges that need to be addressed, but the truth is, this is the greatest country in the world. We have to stop taking it for granted, and make a commitment to keep it the greatest country there is. I truly love and support this country and will do everything in my power to make sure that my children have the opportunity to know how fortunate they are to live in the good ole U.S.A.

Of course, there was a time when we were not allowed to participate in certain things, but that was then and this is now. Now ask yourself honestly: Is there something I've been wanting to do but I talked myself out of it because I believed only white people did it?

Here are some examples of some things that I've heard brothers say only white people do:

1. Become billionaires
2. Surf
3. Scuba dive
4. Rock climb
5. Snow ski
6. Participate in gymnastics
7. Skydive
8. Have monogamous relationships
9. Enjoy nature
10. Travel around the world
11. Exercise
12. Go to therapy
13. Meditate
14. Play golf
15. Enjoy classical music
16. Enjoy the Arts and Theatre
17. Get their Ph.D.
18. Go to spiritual retreats
19. Start their own company
20. Write positive motivational books

Take a moment and ask yourself if there is something on this list that you've really wanted to do but talked yourself out of it because you were afraid of being labeled a sellout. Of course, that list could go on forever, so think about some things that you've stayed away from. Ask yourself right now: "Is there something I've really wanted to do but I talked myself out of it because I was afraid of being rejected by my peers? Have I been afraid of being labeled a 'Sellout' by my brothers and therefore let my dreams float away?"

Is there a part of you that's been saying "Go for it!"? Don't worry what other people think, just do it! If you feel something move inside, you're on the right track. There is a part of you that knows you've got great potential. The key is trust to yourself and that still small voice within you, not the people around you.

Sometimes it only takes a little nudge and then a person will allow himself or herself to take a risk and follow their heart. I hope you will trust your own instincts.

I believe the biggest sellout is the man who allows other people to dictate what he can or cannot do. A "sellout" is someone who is more concerned with looking good in front of his peers rather than following his heart and chasing his dream.

~~~~~~~~~~~~

So, let's be clear: it does not mean that a black man is attempting to be white if he chooses to speak properly and wants to be committed to his education; if he chooses to become a billionaire and has mentors who are white; if he chooses to invest in personal development programs facilitated by white people; by being a loving husband/partner who isn't afraid to show affection to the person he loves out in public because he chooses not to spank his kids as he doesn't believe in corporal punishment because he chooses to be a Republican because he goes to a predominately white church that has a philosophy that truly nurtures his soul.

The CWBS might have you believe that these are things only *white* people do, but none of these things is race-specific. They are choices created by a human being's decision to better himself and a black man should not be accused of trying to be white if he chooses to do any of these things.

Be sure to awaken from this illusion and do not allow anyone or anything to stop you from doing anything your mind and heart tell you to do. Let go of the need to classify anything as black or white. Simply trust and follow your own heart and allow it to guide you to the best things you can do for yourself.

"I am an invisible man...I am a man of substance, of flesh and bone, fiber and liquids—and I might even be said to possess a mind. I am invisible, understand, simply because people refuse to see me."

- Ralph Ellison
Invisible Man

Illusion #4
Black Men Are Less Intelligent

Ever since black people were brought to this country the CWBS has done everything it could to prove that black people were somehow less intelligent than whites. There were (and still are) so-called 'experts' that attempt to prove that we were genetically inferior based on science. There were organizations that proposed that black people had smaller brains than white people and were therefore incapable of being as smart as whites. Even today, there are still a lot of people who argue the case that we are intellectually inferior.

Although times have changed for the better and we have made great strides in race relations in this country, there is still the implied stereotype that black men are *less intelligent* than other men.

Why is that?

I believe it begins with the CWBS. When it comes to reporting stories about black men, the media will accentuate high school dropout rates and how some black males can't read at the same levels of white people. They will seldom show you the black males who are defying the odds and are graduating college and becoming doctors, lawyers, and scientists. In their eyes, good news isn't news. They always want to focus on negativity and sensationalism. I remember listening to a reporter who once said she was instructed to always find the most illiterate and least-educated black person she could find whenever she conducted an interview in the inner city. This instruction is carried out in a lot of cases, whether it is admitted or not. The media will generally showcase the person who least reflects the *true* black experience. It's not that we aren't able to intelligently and articulately express ourselves to the media, it's the fact the media simply chooses not to showcase those of us who can refute claims that we are less intelligent.

So, let's set the record straight. If you look at this country's history, it shouldn't be a stretch to understand why black people, in general, have been stereotyped as less intelligent than other groups. To refute this idea let's begin with a couple of really simple questions.

Question one: *How can black people be expected to be as smart as white people when we were brought to a foreign country and not given access to learn how to read and have equal access to the US educational systems?*

Question two: *Once we did receive access, how can we be expected to compete with whites when we were placed in an inferior educational system that was based on wealth and* *segregation, which left us with inferior schools and, in a lot of cases, unmotivated teachers?*

I'm reminded of a lesson my grandfather taught me when I was about ten years old. I had an experience at school in which a white female classmate of mine made the comment that she was smarter than me because she said her parents told her that white people were smarter than black people. When I shared this with my grandfather this is what he said:

> "I want you to imagine that there are two people about to run a race, both people run at exactly the same speed, so if both people run at exactly the same speed when the race is finished they would end in a tie. But if one of them had a head start, then they would finish first. That is the only difference between black people and white people: they have simply had a head start, but rest assured black people are pretty fast and before you know it black people will catch up with white people and the race will end in a tie."

His words of wisdom really stuck with me and I have used this story to help me deal with the challenges of being a black man in America. It is this simple story that infuses me with the hope and optimism that eventually we will overcome all challenges we face and ultimately we will tie the race as equals. Our goal has never been to try to prove that we are superior - our goal has simply been to be accepted as equals.

My point here is simple: blacks have never been less intelligent than whites, we simply did not have access to the same resources that would have proven our intelligence. Now that we have adequate access to education and information, it is incumbent upon us to make sure that we are taking advantage of this access.

It's been said that if a person does not want to learn, no one can help them, but if a person does want to learn, no one can stop them. We must accept that the media will continue to focus their attention on a small minority of us who appear to be less intelligent. They will focus on some rappers who may not be able to intelligently articulate their point of view, or they will showcase the black man who may not be able to enunciate and pronounce certain words. Either way, the media will continue to focus their attention on the small minority of us, while the majority of us are intelligent, hard-working individuals who simply want to be seen as equal to others.

Since my intention with this book is to help eradicate the ten most destructive media generated illusions about black men, I would like to share a few things we can do to ensure that, despite what the CWBS may do or say, we can still position ourselves for success and not act consistent with the negative stereotypes.

The first thing we must do is to change the mindset of black men and encourage them to embrace the importance of education. I'm reminded of one of my favorite quotes from my favorite scientist, Albert Einstein. *"Education is not the learning of facts, it's rather the training of the mind to think."*

Therefore, our goal should be the *training of the mind to think*. Another important quote that I want you to remember is by self-help guru Anthony Robbins: *"The only true security in life is knowing that every single day you know you are improving yourself in some way."*

These are words to live by and it's important for us to heed them.

The next thing we can do is be willing to look in the mirror and ask ourselves what we can do to ensure that our young men are ready and willing to learn.

I'd like to share another story from my own life that speaks to an issue that we seldom speak about as black men. It's a story of how I "dumbed down" my intelligence to make friends. I'm not sure how prevalent this is in our community, but it's important that we discuss it if we want our young men to embrace education without the fear of losing their identities and their friends.

When I was six years old, I had to live with my father because my oldest sister had a brain tumor and was dealing with lots of health issues. My parents had divorced when I was extremely young and I had no memory of my father, so making this transition was extremely difficult.

Being separated from my mom at such an early age was emotionally and psychologically devastating. Even today I can still feel the sadness of the abandonment I felt because of the separation. When my mother was about to drop me off and leave, she sat me down and made me promise that I would do well in school. She promised me that she would come and pick me up as soon as my sister got better, and it was important for me to get good grades. I promised her that I would and I told her to promise me that she was going to come back and pick me up as soon as possible. She promised she would and she gave me a hug and a kiss and we said goodbye.

Without question, it was the most painful experience of my life. I remember running behind her car as she drove off, screaming, *"please don't leave me, momma. Please don't leave me!"* In retrospect, I have come to realize that it was this event that would shape my life forever.

It turned out that my father lived with his mother, my grandmother. Unfortunately, she hated my mother and blamed her for my parents' divorce. She was a raging alcoholic who took out all her anger and frustrations on me. The environment was abusive and toxic. Try to imagine the worst childhood a child could have and multiply it by ten and you will know what my childhood was like.

The good news is I found refuge in school. I loved going to school and I excelled immediately. I became a straight-A student and I remember having at least three years of perfect attendance. Since my mother had told me that I needed to get good grades, I thought that it would mean she would pick me up sooner. Every time I received a report card I would mail it to her to let her know I was getting good grades. I had hoped that my grades would expedite her picking me up, but unfortunately, it took a lot longer than I had hoped.

After three years I was beginning to lose hope. I started to believe that she would never pick me up. Things at home were getting worse and I was experiencing every type of abuse imaginable.

But I still had my refuge. I still had school.

As fate would have it, there was a teacher named Ms. Bussey who, in some ways, actually saved my life. She saw the potential in me and always challenged me to excel. She also noticed the scars and alerted the school about the physical abuse. Her intervention helped to some degree, but unfortunately, it never lasted for long.

But I stayed focused and strong and kept my promise to my mom to get good grades. I won lots of awards for reading and spelling and was the brightest kid in my class.

After seven long years, my mother was finally able to pick me up and take me home - without question, it was the happiest day of my life.

During the time I was separated from my mom I had absolutely no friends. I was a loner who would spend most of my time alone reading books or playing with some of the animals we lived with.

Once I moved back home with my mom everything changed. I was no longer in a violent environment and I was surrounded by lots of friends for the first time in my life. I was now a teenager and it was important for me to have friends. We lived in government housing and there was something that most of us had in common. Many of us did not have fathers in the house. Without question, this had an impact on our lives. Most of us did not have good male role models to follow, so we sort of followed society's version of masculinity, which unfortunately led us down the wrong path.

I'm sad to say that most of my friends were not good students. As a matter of fact, they rejected school and saw intelligent kids as nerds or that they were pretending to be white. Since my friends were so important to me I decided to "dumb down" and not let them know how much I loved going to school and learning. I started skipping school and hanging out with my friends because for the first time in my life I felt like I had people who really cared about me and I had a social circle that I fit in to. They were my family in some ways, and there was no way that I would reject them.

By the time I got to high school I was so disinterested in school that I was already figuring out how to drop out. When I was in the eleventh grade I went to a seminar and this facilitator convinced me that I could get rich selling vacuum cleaners. I decided to drop out of high school and pursue my dreams of becoming rich, which was obviously a very bad decision.

As mentioned previously, despite me dropping out of school I was able to climb the corporate ladder and become successful. The reason I could do this was because of my love of learning and my willingness to train my mind to think. Herein lies the key to my success. I was willing to educate myself, despite my lack of a formal education.

It is imperative we engage our black men in a conversation about education, not just formal education, but *self-education*. We must impress upon them the importance of constant and never-ending improvement and personal development. We must give them support systems that encourage them to be smart and intelligent without the fear of rejection or being called a sellout.

To do this, it is important for our black males to be exposed to black male educators. According to the U.S. Department of Education, black male teachers make up **only 2%** of teachers in America. I personally believe that having more black male teachers will not only help black male students but those of all races because it will expose them to a side of black men they may not have seen before. It will allow them to experience them as caring, intelligent, compassionate, and empathetic people instead of the negative media-generated stereotypes of being less intelligent, angry, non-caring, and lazy.

Another component would be exposing our black males to positive male role models and mentors. The CWBS would have you believe there is a lack of black male role models. Nothing could be further from the truth. There has always been, and will continue to be, positive black male role models. What is missing is the exposure and media coverage of positive black male role models. But we can no longer wait or rely on the CWBS to showcase the positive role models. It is incumbent upon us to ensure we are making ourselves available and on the front lines empowering our youth and motivating them to reach their full potential.

When it comes to educating our youth, I believe the number one priority we must have is being aware of how important the first seven years of a child's life is. We must understand that these first years shapes his perception of himself and will dictate how well he learns and develops. This can be extremely difficult because there are some people who assume there is a "black" way to raise a child and a "white" way to raise a child. Let me emphasize that this simply isn't true.

As mentioned in a previous chapter, a human mind works like a video recorder. It simply records everything and creates "tapes" of its experiences. As a child gets older, everything is processed through the information stored on those inner tapes. When a child is born into a loving, nurturing, supportive environment and is taught that they are lovable, intelligent, confident, and unique, their tapes reflect this and they become happy whole human beings. When a child is born into a violent, dysfunctional, non-trusting, and non-supportive environment and is taught that they are unloved, stupid, and worthless, these are the tapes through which they live their lives and it will be difficult for them to succeed.

The CWBS would have you believe that the loving, nurturing, and supportive environment is the "white" way to raise a child and the violent, dysfunctional, and non-supportive environment is the "black" way. The fact is it has nothing to do with *race* and everything to do with *environment*. It is the *environment* that shapes our children's beliefs about themselves and the *environment* sets the stage for whether or not our children learn to love themselves and have high self-esteem.

On several occasions, I have witnessed black people say that they were beaten as children and yet they turned out okay. They are in complete denial of the fact that in most cases they really aren't okay, and the sins of the parents are being passed down to the children. I've seen black parents humiliate their children on social media by showing videos of them beating their children to teach them a lesson. I've even heard black "expert" psychologists say that it is okay to physically abuse your child. So for the record, let me say that it's **not okay**. It is never okay to physically or verbally abuse your child. We must understand that words can hit as hard as a fist and the emotional and psychological scars they leave will have a negative impact on that child for the rest of their life.

There is a direct correlation between a child's emotional and intellectual health. If a child feels comfortable and confident about themselves it will be reflected in their ability to learn and to grow. If a child has low self-esteem and does not feel good about themselves they will definitely struggle academically and socially. I will speak more about this in an upcoming chapter.

Since the intention of this chapter is to eradicate the illusion that black men are less intelligent than other men I would like to speak directly to you about ways to ensure you are not acting consistent with that stereotype.

Let's begin by making the distinction between *knowledge* and *opinion*.

Have you ever hung out at a barbershop and engaged in a debate about a particular topic? For example, have you ever debated about who is better: Michael Jordan or LeBron James? Maybe you discussed the current president and whether or not he's a racist. Or maybe you discussed women. Maybe you argued that all women simply want men for their money. If you've never engaged in a heated discussion at a barbershop you are definitely missing out on one of life's greatest pleasures. I love listening to heated debates in barbershops. It always amazes me just how lively and passionate the conversations become.

When it comes to intelligence and knowledge it's important for us to understand that our opinions are not necessarily *knowledge*. People often confuse opinion with fact. For example, if I say all white people are racists, that's an opinion, not a fact. Yet some people will argue with you and say that it is, in fact, a fact. Truth be told, it is still only an opinion. When we present our opinions as facts, we are usually defending a stereotype, which means we are defending an unconscious subconscious belief about a person or a thing.

On the other hand, knowledge is based on fact and replicable information that is irrefutable. A truly intelligent person can separate opinion from fact and they are willing to admit when their opinion might be wrong.

If your only source of information is television media and the barbershop, it's possible that your life is driven by opinions instead of facts, and this perception will likely keep you from experiencing life the way it is meant to be experienced. If you are truly committed to experiencing an extraordinary life you are going to need to invest in increasing your knowledge about yourself and the world around you.

This is why you must commit to constant and never-ending improvement in all areas of your life.

Over the past 28 years, I have read literally hundreds of books, attended hundreds of hours of seminars, listened to hundreds of hours of audio programs, and invested thousands of dollars into my personal growth and development. As a result, I have gained the knowledge to become genuinely happy with myself and my life.

I now coach others to do the same through my books, lectures, online radio show, and a wide variety of other methodologies.

If I only had my opinions to work with I would never have been able to support and empower others. My point is, it is up to **you** to decide that you are going to gain the knowledge you need to live your dreams and you are definitely not going to be held back by other people's opinions.

When I first started writing there were lots of well-meaning people who had the opinion that black men could not succeed writers and speakers. I chose not to listen to their opinions and instead I chose to gain the knowledge I needed to do the things I knew I was capable of doing.

Rest assured that if you are reading this right now you already have everything you need to accomplish anything you want in life. But to do so you must be willing to gain the knowledge and the wisdom to get you to where you want to go.

You have an infinite capacity for learning. All that is needed is your commitment to your own growth and a willingness to do whatever it takes to create the life of your dreams.

My suggestion to you right now is to let go of your opinions and the opinions of others and gain the knowledge you need to do exactly what you were put on this planet to do.

It's all within your reach right now - all you have to do is be willing to grab it.

So grab it!

"Healing begins where the wound was made."

- Alice Walker
The Way Forward Is with a Broken Heart

Illusion #5

Black Men Are Angry and Violent

Have you ever noticed how a lot of black men featured in the media are shown as angry and violent? When was the last time you saw a black man in the news talking about being joyful and happy with a smile on his face?

The media-generated perception is that black men have a greater propensity for violence, yet there is really no scientific evidence that substantiates this belief. As a life coach, I have coached men of all ethnicities and I am absolutely convinced that there is no correlation between race and violence. Violence is driven by the human emotion of anger and emotions transcend race or ethnicity.

The reason so many people accept this negative stereotype is because the CWBS has generally showcased black men as violent and angry.

To make my point, I would like to share an article written by Rachel Grace for the University of Georgia's online newspaper titled *The Red & Black* September 16, 2016.

"Historically, news outlets play into racial stereotypes in attempts to sensationalize their stories and bolster their views and ratings. This can be seen in the coverage of recent protests against police brutality in Ferguson, Baltimore and Baton Rouge, when the media used words such as, "riots," "mobs" and "violence," to describe the actions of the protestors.

"This sort of biased coverage cast a shadow over the true purpose of these demonstrations, and further perpetuated prejudice stereotypes in already tense times for race relations.

"Though there were instances of violence and vandalism at many of these protests, the media does not fairly cover similar acts of violence and vandalism committed by large groups of white people, such as the riots at the Pumpkin Festival in Keene, New Hampshire, and riots following sporting events and decisions, such as when Lane Kiffin resigned from his coaching position for the University of Tennessee in 2010 and a West Virginia University Mountaineers victory in 2014.

"In fact, news outlets often describe these gatherings as being 'rowdy,' 'immature' or as 'misbehavior.'"

This sort of stratified coverage is affecting the public's perception of black Americans. A study by the Public Religion Research Institute showed, *"67 percent of white Americans believe protesting against the government's unfair practices are good for the nation,"* that number dropping to 48 percent when this group was asked the same question, but about black protestors.

University of Georgia students are not in the dark about this issue. Here are some of them weighing in:

"When news covers sports riots as 'parties gone wild,' and black lives matter protests as 'riots,' it justifies the violent actions of white people when it's about sports, while trivializing the black life that was taken. The media love jumping to conclusions and dramatizing situations while they're still breaking, for example, during the Dallas shooting, there was a black man with a gun helping the cops find the actual shooter, but the media reported that he was the killer, simply because he was a black man with a gun."

— Sestina Real, a senior African studies and women's studies double major

"If the media only shows black protests in a negative light, that is all people will know — you have to cover all angles fairly. New outlets should practice total transparent, but it is also our job to hold them accountable. You have to educate yourself outside of the news so you can recognize when something isn't being presented fairly. If you don't ever question the media, it will become your reality."

— Suman Barat, a junior biology and women's studies double major

"Media corporations hold a unique role in modern society, they have the power to influence the public perception on a variety of topics, but there is great responsibility in this. Unfortunately, some news outlets make generalizations about groups of people based on the color of their skin, specifically the black community, in order to boost ratings. The challenge is to seek out unbiased sources, rather than to blindly listen to everything we hear."

— Sai Nagula, a junior biochemistry and molecular biology major

~~~~~~~~~~~~~

Sai Nagula summed it up perfectly in stating; *"Unfortunately, some news outlets make generalizations about groups of people based on the color of their skin, specifically the black community, in order to boost ratings."*

This is exactly what the CWBS does. In order to boost ratings, it focuses on sensationalizing stories by making generalizations about groups of people based on their skin color. In other words, the CWBS perpetuates the illusion that black men are violent and angry because the media knows that's what its customers want to see.

The sad part is that far too many of our black males buy into this stereotype, and they put on these masks of being hard, rigid and tough when in reality they can be sad, scared, or confused.

Generally speaking, regardless of race, men have been conditioned to believe that it's not OK to feel. From a very young age, we are taught that big boys/real men don't cry or show emotion because that is a sign of weakness.

Herein lies the real problem. When we teach our young men to disconnect from their emotions and feelings, it removes their ability to create intimacy and connection with others, which leads to unhealthy relationships. In order to be relational, a man must first be emotional and this is the only way for a man to create authentic fulfilling relationships.

Too many black men are not emotionally equipped to create an authentic connection in relationships, and a lot of this is the result of accepting the media-generated stereotypes that suggest black men are always angry.

So, let's set the record straight: black men do not have a monopoly on anger or violence. We have the same feelings and emotions of any other group of men. We are definitely capable of creating emotionally connected and intimate relationships that truly nurture us. We feel love and compassion, sadness and disappointment, joy and sorrow, we feel empathy and experience true intimacy. Once again, I state we are no different than any other group of men despite what the CWBS may show you through the media.

Our goal must be to redefine masculinity and support our men in understanding their emotions and how to express them appropriately. We must create safe environments that allow men to be OK with being vulnerable, and open their hearts and share their emotions. Creating a dialogue with men about how they feel and then providing them with tools to express their emotions honestly and authentically is the only way we will move past the negative stereotypes that say all black men are violent. So, rest assured that this is the erroneous illusion about black men and the majority of us are not angry and violent and we are definitely capable of expressing our deepest feelings and emotions.

To make a point, I would like to share an important article

that was written in response to the mass shooting that occurred on October 1, 2017, in Las Vegas. Sadly, 58 people lost their lives and 489 others were injured. The article addresses an unspoken fact about men and violence and its message is applicable to men of all ethnicities. The article was written by Charlie Hoehn and was posted on a social media website called Medium.

Ironically, the media perpetuates the illusion that black men are more violent than white men, and yet white men perpetuate the overwhelming majority of mass shootings. Instead of debating which race is more violent, it's important for us to try to find solutions to the violence. I believe this article is a great start.

So take a few minutes and read the article and see if you can relate to the points the author is making.

Thoughts on Vegas and Why Men Keep Doing This.

I'll never forget April 20th, 1999.

I was 12 years old, sitting in art class in middle school. We were playing with clay and making sculptures.

Suddenly, our principal came on over the PA. Her voice trembled.

"I have an important announcement to make. All teachers and students need to hear this. I will wait 60 seconds for everyone to be completely silent."

The next minute was eerie. My friends and I exchanged confused looks, and nervously laughed. Our teacher held her finger to her lips. Silence.

The principal's voice came back onto the PA:

"There is a shooting at Columbine high school. All students are to go home immediately."

Columbine was 15 minutes away from us.

I remember taking the bus home, and walking into my house. My mom turned on the news. I recognized that fence. *We've driven by that fence.*

My mom knew the teacher. Dave Sanders. She'd substituted with him at Columbine.

In the last 18 years, we Americans have experienced too many of these shootings. And I want to share a few of my thoughts on why I think they keep happening.

By the way, this isn't a political post about guns or the media. It's a post about men and their emotional health.

Over the past few years, I've found myself in the mental health space. I've learned a lot. Particularly that men in the United States REALLY struggle in this realm, and have very little social or emotional support. This affects men of every race and socioeconomic background.

I was watching Jimmy Kimmel's impassioned, raw speech last night about the Vegas shootings. Like Jimmy, I felt sick and heartbroken by the tragedy. But something he said stood out to me:

"There's probably no way to ever know why a human being could do something like this to other human beings."

Sadly, researchers know a lot about why human beings—particularly men—do things like this.

1. Men in the United States are chronically lonely.

Boys in the United States—just like all human beings—need touch, caring, warmth, empathy, and close relationships. But as we grow up, most of us lose those essential components of our humanity.

What's worse: we have no idea how to ask for those things or admit we need them, because we're afraid it will make us look weak.

As a man, you might be thinking, "Not me, I've got drinking buddies. I play poker with the guys. I've got friends."

But do you have *confidants?* Do you have male friends who you can actually be vulnerable with? Do you have friends whom you can confide in, be 100% yourself around, who you can hug without saying "No homo," without feeling tense or uncomfortable while you're doing it?

For many men, the answer is "no." So, we spend our time posturing instead.

From an early age, we have an unhealthy ideal of masculinity that we try to live up to. Part of that ideal tells us that ***Real men do everything on their own. Real men don't cry. Real men express anger through violence.***

The byproduct is isolation. Most men spend the majority of their adult lives without deeper friendships or any real sense of community. Not to mention a complete inability to release anger or sadness in a healthy way.

There is a fantastic documentary called *The Mask You*

Live In, which explains how boys in our society are ultimately shaped into mentally unstable adults. My friend Ryan recommended this film to me, after confiding that he cried throughout the entire thing. I cried, as well.

Simon Sinek echoed similar insights on Glenn Beck's show:

"We're seeing a rise of loneliness and isolation. No one kills themselves when they're hungry; we kill ourselves when we're lonely. And we act out, as well.

In the 1960s, there was one school shooting.
In the 1980s, there were 27.
In the 1990s, there were 58.
In the past decade, there have been over 120.

It has nothing to do with guns, it has to do with people feeling lonely.

How do we combat the loneliness that kids are feeling? All of them attacked people in their own community, and all of them attack people they blamed for their own loneliness."

This loneliness compounds as men grow older.

Without deeper friendships or a strong sense of community, the isolation is soul-deadening and maddening. *You are alone.*

Any slight from someone you care about can feel emotionally traumatizing. After enough rejections and feeling like an outcast, you begin to believe that people are just cruel and not worth the effort. You perceive people as threats.

And the effects on our health are devastating. Here is Dr. Dean Ornish, the founder of the Preventive Medicine Research Institute, on the effects of loneliness:

"I am not aware of any other factor—not diet, not smoking, not exercise, not stress, not genetics, not drugs, not surgery—that has a greater impact on our incidence of illness, and [chance of] premature death."

Before we ask, *"How could he do such a thing?"* we have to understand how that person felt on a daily basis, and how those feelings grew over the years.

2. Men in the United States are deprived of play opportunities.

You might be offended by this suggestion.

How could this guy talk about play after a shooting?! Play is for kids!

Wrong.

Homo sapiens play more than any other species. It's impossible to prevent a human from playing. We play shortly after we are born, and the healthiest (and least stressed) humans tend to play for their entire lives.

Play may be God's greatest gift to mankind. It's how we form friendships, and learn skills, and master difficult things that help us survive. Play is a release valve for stress and an outlet for creativity. Play brings us music, comedy, dance, and everything we value.

Above all, play is how we bond with each other—it's how we communicate "I am safe to be around, I am not a threat." Play is how we form connections with other humans.

The irony is that loneliness would not be a problem if we all got ample time to play. Not only would we have deeper friendships, we'd also have better relationships *with ourselves.* Play allows us to enjoy our own company.

There is a strong correlation with play deprivation and mental illness.

When you deprive mammals of play, it leads to chronic depression. When you deprive a human child of play, their mental and emotional health deteriorate. Play suppression has enormous health consequences.

"But the Vegas shooter loved to gamble! He went on cruises!"

That's not the type of play I'm talking about.

To better understand this dynamic, we need to look at the background of another mass shooter.

In 1966, Charles Whitman shot his wife and mother. Then, he climbed up the tower at the University of Texas in Austin, and shot 46 people. In total, he murdered 16 people. At the time, this was the biggest mass shooting of its kind in United States history.

Dr. Stuart Brown and his team of researchers were commissioned to find out what "The Texas Sniper" had in common with other mass murderers.

They gained a key insight when they examined their childhoods.

Brown recalls:

> *"None of them engaged in healthy rough-and-*

tumble play. The linkages that lead to Charles Whitman producing this crime was an unbelievable suppression of play behavior throughout his life by a very overbearing, very disturbed father."

Healthy and joyful play must be had in order to thrive. Boys need to wrestle with their dads, and they need to roughhouse with other boys. Parents and teachers need to play with their kids.

But more importantly, they need to encourage those kids to *go out and play.* And then, let them be.

"It's 10 o'clock. Do you know where your kids are?"

Ever since that famous ad aired, parents have shamed each other into watching their kids like a hawk.

If you let your kid walk up the street alone, you'll either get a call from another parent, or the cops will pick them up. Our kids are stripped of their right to experience life on their own terms.

In an effort to improve our kids' test scores and beef up their future resumes, we've stripped away nearly all of their free play opportunities. Recess has been sacrificed in the name of Scantrons, and pills are prescribed to the kids whose bodies and minds cry out for play.

The result: A generation of the most anxious, depressed, and suicidal American children on record.

This is in alignment with Dr. Peter Gray's research, who studied the epidemic of mental illness and the decline in play:

"Over the past half century, in the United States and other developed nations, children's free play with other

children has declined sharply. Over the same period, anxiety, depression, suicide, feelings of helplessness, and narcissism have increased sharply in children, adolescents, and young adults... **The decline in play has contributed to the rise in the psychopathology of young people."**

This is why I believe mental illness may be the biggest health crisis of our lifetimes. Because those kids will grow up into isolated adults who don't know how to play, or seek out their friends when they are lonely. They have no emotional support.

They are alone.

~~~~~~~~~~

In the most memorable chapter of *So You've Been Publicly Shamed*, the author describes the research of James Gilligan, a young psychiatrist at Harvard Medical School in the 1970s.

Gilligan was invited to make sense of the Massachusetts's prisons and mental hospitals, where he interviewed murderous inmates. He included in his notebook this heartbreaking observation:

"They would all say that they themselves had died before they started killing other people... They felt dead inside. They had no capacity for feelings. No emotional feelings. Or even physical feelings.

Universal among the violent criminals was the fact that they were keeping a secret. A central secret. And that secret was that they felt ashamed— deeply ashamed, chronically ashamed, acutely ashamed.

I have yet to see a serious act of violence that was not

provoked by the experience of feeling shamed or humiliated, disrespected and ridiculed."

ALL OF US will face difficult times in our lives where we will experience shame, humiliation, disrespect, and ridicule.

Do you know what gets us through those hard times?

Friendship: The love and support you get, from the people you play with.

I don't know much about the Vegas shooter. Maybe he was an evil psychopath (like Eric Harris). Maybe he had a psychotic break from pharmaceutical drugs.

Whatever the case, these factors about mass shooters are often true:

1. They are deeply lonely. They have no significant friendships to rely on, and very few quality people to confide in.

2. They experienced ongoing play deprivation. Their innate ability was crippled, and they struggle to maintain a healthy emotional connection with themselves and others.

3. They are deeply ashamed. They experienced extreme ridicule, rejection, or humiliation.

Are there other factors at play here?

Absolutely. Mass shootings are complex, and so are people. They don't fit perfectly into our narratives.

Do the above three factors always lead to murderous behavior?

Of course not. But over time, they destroy an individual's emotional health. And that's the point.

We've created a culture where the first two factors — loneliness and play deprivation — affect *everyone.* And because friendship struggles to take root in this environment, we are more likely to be struck by the third factor — shame.

Even though we're in the safest period in the history of civilization, these shootings will keep happening in America. They happen every single day. Guns are a part of the problem, and so is the media. But there is a bigger problem:

We are a culture that continually neglects the emotional health of our boys, and our men.

The good news is that you, as an individual, can make a difference.

Reach out to someone who you think could be lonely, and invite them to do something fun together. Keep inviting them. Build trust, and confide in each other. Set the example by being a safe and supportive person to be around.

If you've noticed their personality has <u>drastically changed</u>, invite them out for several hours. Be there for them. Encourage them to get professional help. You could save their life.

~~~~~~~~~~~~

This sentence summarizes the entire point of this chapter:

"We are a culture that continually neglects the emotional

health of our boys and our men."

For more than 25 years, I have been writing and speaking about men's issues and everything I have learned can be summed up in this one sentence. There is a lot of emphasis these days on mental health and the problems it causes, but I will assert that it isn't mental health, but *emotional* health that is our greatest challenge. It's been said that the longest journey a man can take is the eighteen inches from his head to his heart. When we speak about mental health, we're speaking about a man's head or intellect. When we speak about emotional health, we're speaking about a man's heart. The time has come for all men to make that 18-inch journey and move from his head to his heart.

In my book *A New Conversation With Men* (Creation Publishing Group 2008), I identified what I called "The Five Illusions of Manhood." These five illusions are what cause the overwhelming majority of pain and suffering in a man's life. The first and most important illusion I discovered was this: ***to be a man you must be non-emotional and disconnected.***

When a man is trapped in this illusion he disconnects from the most important aspect of his humanity, which are his feelings and emotions. Our current culture of masculinity has promoted this idea since the caveman days. From the very beginning, men were taught that they had two primary responsibilities: to provide and to protect. This strategy worked well for hundreds of years, however, it definitely does not work in the evolved world in which we currently live. What most of us as men were never taught was how important it is to learn how to connect. In order to connect, a man must be in touch with his feelings and emotions, but, because of the first illusion, most men aren't comfortable doing this.

Without question, emotions transcend race or ethnicity. My experience with doing men's work is that the current paradigm of masculinity is breaking down and more and more men are beginning to open up to these new ideas. Unfortunately, I have found reluctance by black men to engage in this dialog. This can be attributed to several factors, such as lack of black males involved in facilitating men's groups, lack of resources targeted specifically to black males to talk about these issues, and religious beliefs. But since you're reading this book right now, this tells me that you are open to new ideas, so now I'd like to explain why it's so important for us as black men to get involved with our emotional healing

I'd like to share a Wikipedia entry about the shooting of Philando Castile. As you read the entry, try to notice how you feel. Most men will be able to tell you what they think, but they aren't able to share how they feel. So after you finish reading the entry, try to tap into the emotion that you feel.

> On July 6, 2016, **Philando Castile** was shot and killed by Jeronimo Yanez, a St. Anthony, Minnesota, police officer, after being pulled over in Falcon Heights, a suburb of Saint Paul. Castile was in a car with his girlfriend, Diamond Reynolds, and her four-year-old daughter when he was pulled over by Yanez and another officer.
>
> The shooting achieved a high profile from a live-streamed video on Facebook made by Diamond Reynolds in the immediate aftermath of the shooting. It

shows her interacting with the armed officer as a mortally injured Castile lies slumped over, moaning slightly and his left arm and side bloody. The Hennepin County Medical Examiner's office said he had sustained multiple gunshot wounds and reported that Castile died at 9:37 p.m. CDT in the emergency room of the Hennepin County Medical Center, about 20 minutes after being shot.

According to a police dashcam video/audio, after being asked for his license and registration, Castile told the officer he had a firearm, to which the officer replied 'Don't reach for it then'. After saying 'Don't pull it out' twice, the officer shot at Castile seven times.

Reynold's testimony was that Castile was shot while reaching for his ID after telling Yanez he was armed.[8]

On November 16, 2016, John Choi, the Ramsey County Attorney, announced that Yanez was being charged with three felonies: one count of second-degree manslaughter and two counts of dangerous discharge of a firearm. Choi said, *"I would submit that no reasonable officer knowing, seeing, and hearing what Officer Yanez did at the time would have used deadly force under these circumstances."*

Yanez was acquitted of all charges on June 16, 2017. The same day, the City of Saint Anthony said it was offering Officer Yanez a voluntary separation agreement.

~~~~~~~~~~~~~

What did you feel as you read the entry? Was it rage? Anger? Sadness? Fear? Anxiety? Confusion? Compassion? Sympathy? What did you feel?

As men who happen to be black, I believe our highest priority should be to encourage each other to get in touch with our emotions and have access to resources that allow us to do so. It is important for us to have outlets to deal with the emotional and psychological trauma we experience on a daily basis. Whether we will admit it or not, the constant barrage of negativity we are exposed to on a daily basis can have a negative impact on our wellbeing. It's important for us to be able to talk openly with others so we can heal the trauma, and we must have safe supportive environments in which to do so.

I'd like to share an article I wrote as a result of the Philando Castile and Alton Sterling murders. I wrote this article as a means to deal with the intense feelings of sadness I was experiencing. It was my way of dealing with the tragedy and my hope was that it would help others deal with the events as well.

Healing the Racial Heart of America

The past few days have been extremely difficult for me as I'm sure it has been for most people. My heart is filled with sadness and I have been withholding tears because I did not want to feel the pain. But today I allowed myself to feel into the sadness, the hurt and the frustration and I'm allowing myself to heal from the hurt. But rest assured it still hurts. The pain runs deep but I will heal.

My heart was broken as I watched the videos of Philando Castile and Alton Sterling have their lives senselessly taken in yet another incident of unnecessary violence. My heart ached as I thought about the trauma

Philando's young daughter and fiancée experienced as they witnessed their loved one lose his life right in front of their eyes. I cannot get the picture of his bloodied body out of my mind. It symbolizes the dehumanization of men of color and the powerlessness we sometimes feel simply because of the color of our skin and it hurts. It really hurts.

I am also deeply saddened that the recent events opens the wounds of racism once again in this country and perpetuates the illusion that it is "us" versus "them" which causes a sense of separation and division in our country. But as painful as it feels right now I remain hopeful that these events can actually become a catalyst that brings us closer together instead of tearing us apart as a nation and in some ways that we may not understand these events are actually necessary to wake this country up.

I've cried because of the emotional and psychological impact these events will have on young black male minds and hearts. Though everyone can feel the hurt and pain of these types of events, too many black males will conclude that their lives don't matter and will simply give up and stop trying, or worse, they will act out in ways that support the negative media generated stereotypes. Which is another thing that brought me pain. The people who say #alllivesmatter show no compassion or empathy for the challenges facing people of color in this country. How can they not see that #blacklivesmatter in no way implies that other lives do not matter. It states the obvious truth that black lives have always been devalued in this country and we have been labeled as inferior since we were brought here. We aren't attempting to be treated as superior but simply as equals because our lives do matter and we are valuable assets to this country not liabilities.

After these two horrific events my heart once again was cracked wide open with pain as several law officers lives were unnecessarily taken in retaliation for the killings. The pain comes from knowing that the overwhelming majority of police officers are actually good cops and should not have to live in fear that their lives will be taken in retaliation of the actions of a few bad ones. Most of them are committed to protect and serve but at the same time I believe it's time for them to address the real problems within their organization. The good cops must not be afraid to call out the bad ones. They must be willing to protect and save us from their own and sometimes that will mean that they break the code of brotherhood within the force to remove the ones who do not deserve to wear the badge.

In no way can I ever justify violence. Violence begets violence and I personally cannot and will not condone it in any form. But I must admit that I also felt a sense of sadness and compassion for Micah Johnson. I definitely did not feel this way because he took the lives of others, but because I can empathize with his pain and anger. It's easy to label a person a monster when they commit these horrendous crimes but if we truly want to rid ourselves of violence we must begin asking ourselves some deeper questions about what causes it in the first place. I do not want to excuse him or try and justify his actions in any way and pretend that he is the victim here because he isn't. Every human being should be held 100% accountable for their actions, but I believe he unfortunately symbolizes how too many black men feel most of the time and that is angry and powerless.

Violent acts in my opinion are never justifiable but without question feeling angry is. A lot of black men are angry and when their anger isn't acknowledged it simply creates more anger. Feeling anger does not mean we hate white people or this country. It means we have been invalidated and abused and it is our way of defending ourselves from that abuse.

As I write these words with tears rolling down my face I recognize that my heart is healing. Sharing these words have helped me process my feelings and I can feel my sadness lifting. I can feel my sense of optimism returning and I am convinced that the best days for this country are ahead of us and not behind us. If I can heal my hurt so too can America.

President Obama was quoted as saying: *"As painful as the week has been, I fully believe that America is not as divided as people have suggested."* I concur with his statement. I do not believe that race relations are getting worse; I believe technology now captures the injustices we've been talking about and experiencing for a very long time. So I am hopeful that the events of the last few days can wake us up and help us start healing the heart of America. It begins by remembering the creed: *"Together We Stand, Divided We Fall".*

It begins with healing our own hearts and if you are white and struggling with what to do about the recent tragedies consider these 2 ideas.

1. Open your heart and have compassion. If you aren't black you may not be able to empathize with the feelings we have but you can have compassion for our feelings. Know that we are justified in our anger and fear and do not invalidate our experience. #blacklivesmatter was never intended to say other lives didn't matter. Its intention was to validate our experience of the violence we receive from police and society as a whole. Just try for a moment to walk in our shoes and know that it is a very difficult walk at times.

2. Be honest with your feelings about black people in general. Have you accepted the negative media generated stereotypes about black people? Are you justifying these killings by saying he was resisting arrest and thereby denying that this is even a problem? Be willing to examine your own hidden judgments and biases about black people and be willing to accept that those judgments might be wrong. Be willing to change your perception about black people and do not be afraid to speak up to people of your ethnicity who may think differently than you do if you're saying things like #blacklivesmatter or recognize the unnecessary violence perpetuated by cops.

If you're black I'd like to offer a few ideas to consider.

First of all know that you are justified in your feelings of anger, sadness, fear or rage. Do not deny how you feel and never let anyone invalidate your feelings. However, you cannot justify violence or hate. Don't buy in to hate. Find a support system that helps you deal with your emotions and provides a safe place for you to express them. Give yourself permission to grieve and heal if that's what you need to do. Healing comes from expressing your feelings with others and allowing whatever emotion you may have to be released. Let go of all negative or painful emotions.

Second, do not accept the media generated idea that it is "us" against "them". Although I do believe some violent acts are racially motivated, I do not believe the majority of white people are racist. I do not believe that our collective society is racist and that white people are attempting to eliminate black people. Without question the system is definitely broken and biased but we cannot continue to promote this idea that it is us against them. There are people of all races working to find solutions to the racial challenges we have in this country and it's going to take all of us to resolve them. As long as you believe it is us against them things will never change. We must work together to heal the heart of America and the world.

Last but definitely not least, **know that there are reasons for optimism** and choose to become an optimist. I recognize that there are lots of challenges facing us and on the surface it might appear that our challenges are insurmountable. However, I believe there are lots of reasons for optimism and I believe that the future is brighter than most people think. One way to become an optimist is to simply disconnect from the media. You must recognize that the media's job is to showcase everything that is wrong with the world. It thrives on negativity and pessimism. Don't buy in to the negative media. I can assure you that there are a lot more things that are right with the world than are wrong with it.

Look for the things that are right. Focus your attention on solutions rather than problems and follow Ghandi's advice and become the change you want to see in the world.

As mentioned, I'm still optimistic about the future. There is always darkness before the dawn and the light of truth always overcomes darkness.

So I will leave you with the beautiful and insightful words of Dr. Martin Luther King Jr; *"Darkness cannot drive out darkness; only light can do that. Hate cannot drive out hate; only love can do that."*

Let's love a lot more!

~~~~~~~~~~~~

For several days after Philando Castile's murder, I was consumed by sadness and grief. I couldn't get the video out of my mind. I kept thinking about the event and my sadness deepened. I tried to shake the sadness but I couldn't. Even today, my heart still hurts for Philando and his family.

Fortunately, I had a support system that allowed me to share my pain and sadness. Three of my closest friends and I were at a meeting discussing a possible collaboration to create an organization called *The Circle of Inclusion and Diversity*. It was a mixed race group of men and women who were coming together to try to create solutions to the violence and hatred that was permeating the country at the time.

At the beginning of the meeting, we each had an opportunity to share how we were feeling about the country as a whole.

When it was my turn to speak, I tried to contain my sadness but the pain was too deep. I began to cry profusely as I shared how broken-hearted I felt as a result of Philando's murder. As I shared my feelings, the pain intensified and was almost unbearable. But I knew I needed to let it go in order to heal. So I did. I allowed myself to feel the deep sadness I had been holding on to for days and after several minutes of crying, the pain began to subside.

The beautiful part about it was how the group allowed me to express the sadness without ridicule or judgment. No one tried to invalidate how I felt or tried to comfort me with words of encouragement. They simply allowed me to feel and express those feelings. By allowing myself to fully feel and express my sadness, I was able to release it and become free from it. It was one of the most healing and transforming experiences of my life.

The moral of this story is it's important for us to be willing to heal our hearts and let go of emotional pain. Life is difficult and we've all been hurt and victimized in some way. It is up to us to take complete responsibility for our emotional wellbeing and be willing to do whatever it takes to be emotionally free.

Black men are not more violent than other men. We have the capacity and the ability to be just as loving, caring, joyful, compassionate, and authentic as any other men. We can no longer accept the CWBS stereotypes and the only way for us to remove them is for us to be willing to do our inner work and heal our own inner pain.

My hope is that this chapter will encourage you to examine your own emotional state of being. I want you to know that the three most difficult words for any man to say are I NEED HELP! There is nothing wrong with uttering these three words. As a matter of fact, it isn't until you become courageous enough to say them that you can begin the process to change. We must remove the stigma of asking for help and recognize that asking for it is actually a sure sign of strength. When we gain the courage to address our emotional selves we will gain the freedom to be who we truly are. Until we do our inner work, we will never have the tools of awareness that can truly set us free.

Your top priority is to be emotionally free. Once you are free, everything else in your life will automatically fall into place. Shoot for freedom!

Relationships are the glue that holds our lives together. We must ensure that we create strong bonds with our mates that are authentic, nurturing, rewarding, and fulfilling. Few things are more important than creating a relationship with the person who happens to be perfect for you.

Coach Michael Taylor

Illusion #6

Black Men Cannot Be Monogamous

Back in the 1970s, the CWBS released a series of films, which later became known as "Blaxploitation" films. The intention of the films was to bring urban culture to white America, but unfortunately, all they did were perpetuate negative stereotypes about black people. Some of the movies portrayed black men as pimps and hustlers that objectified women and glorified infidelity. These were the role models we were exposed to, and unfortunately too many of us began to emulate their negative behavior.

During the 1980s, rap music began to dominate the airwaves and once again a flurry of negative stereotypes about black men permeated the culture. Black men were perceived to be sex-crazed materialistic hoodlums who only thought of making money and having sex. We were bombarded with black men promoting the idea of being a "playa" who slept with as many women as possible and had no emotional attachment. One rapper expressed this sentiment with these words to a very popular rap song: *"I am into having sex I'm not into making love."*

Even today, we are bombarded with negative images of black men as unable to commit to one woman and unwilling to create loving monogamous relationships.

For the record, I believe every human being is 100% responsible for their actions. The media cannot make a person do something. No one is holding a gun to our heads making us do something we don't want to do. We must accept responsibility for the consequences of our actions and know that our greatest gift as human beings is the power to choose. Therefore, we must choose not to act consistent with the negative media-generated stereotypes.

However, imagery can definitely influence a person's behavior, and in the case of black men and negative media, it has definitely contributed to some of us acting consistent with those stereotypes.

Let me reiterate the intention of this book, *"I want to dispel the negative media-generated stereotypes about black men. To do this, I must begin by having a conversation with you. That's right, this book is written specifically for you."*

So let's begin with you.

Do you believe it's possible for a black man to remain monogamous? Are you capable of being monogamous? It's not my place to judge you or condemn you for your beliefs. My job is to challenge you to think about the unconscious subconscious beliefs you have about a person or thing. What are your beliefs about black men? Can they be monogamous? Can you?

There is no shortage of opinions in regard to men and monogamy. So I would like to share my opinions about why I believe in monogamy and why I am committed to it.

So, let's begin with why some men do not believe monogamy is possible. In our current paradigm of masculinity, men are conditioned to believe that sexual conquest is the only true gauge of manhood. This is actually the second illusion that I wrote about in my book *A New Conversation With Men*. Because of this illusion, a lot of men think that the more women they sleep with, the more they validate their masculinity. This illusion is not limited to just black men. Men of all races and ethnicities fall victim to this illusion.

It is this illusion that causes men to act out sexually and try to prove their manhood through sexual conquests. For men who are trapped in this illusion, the thought of being faithful to one woman is a blow to their ego. The truth is, their fear of settling down with one woman is actually triggered by their fear of being unlovable. Men may not admit this, but the truth is if we are unable to love ourselves it is impossible to love someone else. And when we don't love ourselves we begin rationalizing ways to get people to love us.

For men who must sleep with multiple women, it's really a matter of trying to fill a void in their hearts where they don't feel good about themselves. By not allowing a single woman to fully love them for who they are, they perpetuate emptiness in their hearts that no amount of sex can ever fill. Of course, their rationalization becomes *"I'm just a playa"*. The truth is, you are just a man who is terrified of being authentically loved by someone and you're using sex as a way to try to feel good about yourself. I am absolutely convinced that infidelity is never about physical sex: it is an attempt to fill an unmet emotional need.

Think of it this way:

When you meet someone for the first time and begin dating you are filled with the feeling of happiness. It's an amazing feeling that causes us to continually think about the person we are having the feelings about. It is this energy or feeling that makes us crave more, so we choose to spend as much time as possible with that person to feel that energy.

Some people call this *the honeymoon stage* and you do not have to be married to experience it.

The reason we are so happy at the beginning is because we are usually wearing our masks (and so are our partners) and hiding behind a lot of fear and anxiety about being accepted by the other person. So at the beginning, we are doing all of these nice things for our partners to keep that good feeling of happiness going.

After being in the relationship for a while, our masks begin to fall off and the real us shows up. This happens to both people. As our masks fall off, we must then deal with all the fears and insecurities we have about ourselves. The only way to do this is by being vulnerable and authentic with your mate, but that is too scary for most people, so they put the masks back on and keep pretending that they are happy.

Unfortunately, relationships are actually designed to help us take off our masks, but too many people are unwilling to do this.

So now you have two people who are pretending to be happy, but because they had begun to take off their masks they can no longer pretend. Once the masks have been taken down, it's no longer possible to pretend that you are happy.

Since most people are unwilling to deal with their insecurities directly, they begin to find fault in their mate as a defense mechanism. All of a sudden, the cute little things they used to do are now annoying as hell and instead of letting them go we cling to them and use them as excuses to pick fights with our partners. By now, that happy energy we felt at the beginning is gone. We have no idea where it went, but the feeling is no longer there. Since we are unwilling to be real and authentic with our mates about our insecurities and theirs, we then decide that we want to get that happy feeling back, so unconsciously we begin looking for a new relationship.

All of a sudden, we meet a new person and we start to feel that happy feeling again. We start spending more time with the new person and we begin rationalizing how happy the new person makes us feel and then we decide that we will leave the old person and hook up with the new one.

And guess what happens? We do the same thing all over again. The new person becomes just like the old person, so we begin looking for a new one to get the happy feeling back.

This becomes a vicious cycle that you can never break until you decide to take off your mask and become real and authentic with yourself and the person you are in a relationship with. The pleasure of physical sex cannot compare to the joy of authentic intimacy. Authentic intimacy isn't possible until you are willing to remove your mask.

Once again, I would like to share a story from my own life to illustrate my point.

As I mentioned earlier, I had a very traumatic childhood. As a result of the trauma, I created a mask called Mr. Nice Guy. While wearing this mask, I always put other people's emotional needs before my own. The psychological term is called being *co-dependent*. While wearing my mask, I made sure that I did everything right for the women in my life. I was a nice, faithful, good-looking guy who wasn't afraid of showing affection and I had no problem being monogamous. When I got married the first time, I had no idea that I was wearing this mask. I did everything I possibly could to be a good husband, but unfortunately, my marriage ended in divorce.

What I learned about myself is I had spent so much time trying to be nice and trying to be the perfect husband that I actually forgot about my emotional needs and myself. After some deep self-introspection and healing, I became aware of the mask I was wearing and I was eventually able to take it off. By being willing to face my inner demons and heal my heart, I learned to be authentic and real with my emotions and it allowed me to develop authentic, emotionally connected relationships. This is why the previous chapter is so important. As men, we must be willing to acknowledge our emotional wounds and be willing to heal them if we want to remove our masks.

As a result of removing my masks, I was able to find the perfect woman for me and I have been blissfully married for the past fifteen years. I know some men will say that I'm whipped and I'll have my "playa" card revoked, but that's okay by me. I absolutely love and adore my wife and I love being married. I love the emotional stability and trust that I have with my wife that really nurtures me and lets me know that I am authentically loved for the man that I am. I love how my wife lights up every time I walk into a room and how she brags about how awesome her husband is with her friends. I love that we are partners and work as a team in all areas of our lives and I can depend on her to be there for me no matter what challenge we have to face. The young folks would call her my *ride or die* chick and I know with absolute certainty that she always has my back.

So, rest assured that all black men are definitely capable of being monogamous, but ultimately all black men may not choose to be. The real question you have to ask yourself is, are you willing to choose monogamy for yourself? Are you open to the possibility that you could create a relationship that is rewarding and fulfilling and fulfill all your emotional, psychological, and spiritual needs? Monogamy is a choice, it has nothing to do with race or ethnicity, it is a choice that involves commitment and openness, vulnerability and a willingness to share ourselves with another in a way that creates a bond that can never be broken. So ultimately you get to choose. Will you choose monogamy?

If the answer is yes, I'd like to share an article I wrote titled **5 Keys To A Loving & Fulfilling Marriage,** which I believe can support you in creating a rewarding and fulfilling marriage or committed relationship. If you are willing to follow these five keys, I am absolutely certain you can create a spiritual partnership of your dreams.

On April 9, 2017, my wife and I celebrated our 15th year wedding anniversary. To celebrate we decided to take a 10-day Mediterranean cruise. It was an amazing experience that I will cherish for the rest of my life. After our cruise, I spent some time reflecting on our marriage and how wonderful it is to share my life with someone who I truly love and appreciate. As I reflected on our marriage that is currently so rewarding and fulfilling, I started thinking about my first marriage, which unfortunately wasn't so wonderful. As I was reliving my first marriage in my mind I begin asking myself why my first marriage didn't work out and yet my second marriage was all that I've dreamed a marriage could be.

The more I thought about it the more I realized that one of the reasons my first marriage failed was because I was trapped in what a "traditional" marriage was supposed to be like. In retrospect, I realized that I was simply following a culturally created script of what marriage was supposed to be like and this script was actually an over-romanticized media generated fantasy that was actually out of touch with reality. In other words, I had gotten married for all the wrong reasons because I was following the "traditional" script of what a marriage was supposed to be.

After spending some extensive time thinking about the differences between my two marriages I decided to share the five most important things I've learned that have helped me create a beautiful spiritual partnership with the woman who is absolutely perfect for me. My hope is that these keys will inspire you to create your own loving and fulfilling relationship/marriage.

So if you're truly ready to create a loving and fulfilling marriage let's get started.

Here are the 5 keys that will lay the foundation for you to create the relationship/marriage of your dreams.

1. Unpack your emotional baggage

It's been documented that the average wedding in the US costs between 5 and 20 thousand dollars. Traditionally, it's been set up that we make this huge investment in our weddings to show how much we love our spouses. But is this true? Does the amount of money we spend on a wedding have anything to do with the marriage itself? If you really stop and think about it the answer is a resounding NO! Traditionally, weddings have been set up to try and impress our family and friends. In reality, they in no way enhance our marriages. As a matter of fact, I would argue that they actually add stress to the marriage because of the financial, emotional and psychological stress they create. If you truly want to enhance your marriage let me suggest that you make an investment in unpacking your emotional baggage.

Let me explain what I mean.

After my divorce, the first words out of my mouth were: "I'll never get married again." The reason I said this was because of the emotional pain I felt as a result of my divorce. At the time, I couldn't identify this pain but I unconsciously began building a wall around my heart that would protect me from experiencing that pain again. After several months the pain subsided and I decided to attempt to at least develop a relationship with someone. Each of my relationships after my divorce was a disaster. They would usually last about three weeks and they would all end with the woman saying, "I care too much about you to stay in this relationship." This made absolutely no sense to me. How could you care about someone and leave him or her at the same time?

After noticing a pattern in my relationships I finally recognized that I was the only common denominator in all of them and I decided that I was the problem, not the women in my life. I then made a commitment to myself that I was going to figure out how to create a great relationship and I knew that I had to look at myself first. I then committed to unpacking my emotional baggage and by far it was the best decision of my life. It began with my willingness to go to therapy and to pinpoint some traumatic events from my childhood that were actually affecting my life as an adult. I learned that I had a deep fear of abandonment, which kept me from trusting anyone out of fear that they would leave me. This was my deepest emotional wound. By healing this wound it allowed me to learn to trust again and the walls around my heart began to fall.

By making the emotional and financial investment to unpack my emotional baggage it allowed me to create the space for true love to come into my life and that is the primary reason that my current marriage works. So the first step in creating a great relationship/marriage is to break tradition and make the investment (emotional and financial) in yourself to make sure that you aren't carrying any baggage that will keep you from loving someone or being loved by someone.

2. Define your personal values and know your non-negotiables.

When I got married the first time I had no idea what my true values were. As I mentioned, I was simply following a societal script that said as a man I was supposed to be married. I had no idea what was truly important to me in terms of qualities and values in a woman. I have since learned that it is important to identify what your core values are and what your non-negotiable attributes are in a relationship.

Here are six values that you must share with a potential partner if you want to create a relationship/marriage that is loving and fulfilling.

Family, Money, Health, Spirituality, Sex and Ambition. Make sure that you are clear on how you feel about each of these values and make sure that your partner shares those same values.

The next thing you must do is come up with a list of 3-5 non-negotiable things that you are unwilling to compromise. This should not be a long drawn out list but it has to be a list of things that you are absolutely unwilling to compromise. Only you know what those things are but it's important that you identify them before you enter into a relationship.

For example, I would never date someone who smoked. It was non-negotiable for me. So when I went on a first date that was one of the first questions I asked. If the person said yes I would know that I didn't want to date that person. I definitely believe in compromising in relationships. But I also know there are some things that I would never ever compromise. So you must decide what your non-negotiables are and make sure that you never compromise them.

3. Let go of traditional roles and responsibilities in the relationship/marriage.

Traditionally we fall victim to certain roles in marriage and relationships. For a very long time, men were taught that our primary roles were to provide and protect. So we followed tradition and found jobs to provide for our families and promised to protect our families from any type of threat that may have shown up in our lives. Women were taught that they were the nurturers and homemakers and they embraced those roles until the feminist movement started and women decided that they wanted to be treated as equals and all of a sudden all the roles begin to change.

If you truly want to create a marriage that works you are going to have to let go of some antiquated roles and embrace the idea that marriage is a spiritual partnership between two equals in which both parties agree that they are a team and neither one is above the other. As a team, they work together in all ways to ensure that their partnership is connected and intimate. It should be a place where each person feels safe and secure to be who they truly are and they are showered with love, appreciation and acceptance.

As a team, it doesn't matter who brings home the bacon, cooks the dinner or cleans the house. It doesn't matter who clothes the kids, pays the bills, or files the taxes. It only matters that each team member is willing to do his or her part in ensuring that the team always wins. This is one of the reasons why my current marriage works. My wife and I have a partnership and we always work together to ensure that our team wins.

4. Listen to your heart and love who you choose to love.

I recently watched a beautiful movie titled Loving which was based on the true story of Richard and Mildred Loving who were an interracial couple that ended up going to the Supreme Court to strike down anti-miscegenation laws in Virginia in 1967. They won the landmark case, which opened the door for all people to marry regardless of race in America. The movie reminded me just how far we've come and how far we still have to go in regards to race in this country. If the Loving's had listened to tradition they would have never been together. But instead, they chose to listen to their hearts and created a beautiful love affair and marriage.

Unfortunately, there are still people who may disagree with interracial marriage and dating. They are locked into the "tradition" that only people of the same race should be together. And of course, this isn't just about race. There are some people who disagree with people of different religions being together. There are others who do not believe people of the same gender should be together.

So what about you? What do you believe?

For me, it's pretty simple. Love transcends race, religion or sexual orientation. Human beings are all the same. What's on the inside definitely transcends what you see on the outside. Feelings are the language of the soul and the soul has no ethnicity. The external traditional labels that society has created do not define who a person truly is. It is their thoughts, feelings, beliefs and actions that define them and that's what human beings fall in love with. It's who they are, not what they are, that connects us.

If you are trapped in the traditional way of thinking, there is the possibility that you will miss out on the opportunity to love and be loved, so break tradition and love who you choose to love. Trust your own heart, not traditions.

5. Make your marriage top priority in your life.

One of the reasons my first marriage failed was because I unknowingly did not make it a priority. I was unaware of this at the time but I thought by being a good husband, providing for my family and loving my kids my marriage would work out. Nothing could be further from the truth. Marriage takes conscious effort. We must be willing to gain the emotional and psychological tools that allow us to create emotional and spiritual connections with our partners.

Traditionally in marriage, if there are challenges we may go to church and speak with ministers to help us get through the tough times. Although I have no problem with this, I have learned that sometimes religion is the actual problem. Religion has passed down some traditional roles that can actually be detrimental to a great marriage. I remember speaking with a minister when I was contemplating getting a divorce from my first wife and the response from the minister was to simply pray about it and God would fix it.

Needless to say, that didn't work. I ended up getting divorced and God couldn't fix it.

But I could. I then decided to take complete responsibility for my happiness and I decided that I was going to figure out how to create a lifelong love affair. I let go of all the traditional antiquated ideas of what marriage was supposed to be and I chose to create a marriage on my own terms. In doing so I ended up creating a soulmate relationship and a spiritual partnership that nurtures and supports me in every way.

If I can do it, so can you. To do so you must break tradition and follow your heart.

Are you willing to do that?

~~~~~~~~~~~~~

Since we're talking about relationships, I thought this would be a good time to share my views on interracial dating.

There is a stereotype that says all successful black men choose to marry white women. This is a stereotype that is easily refuted by simply looking at the statistics from the US Census that says 73% of black men marry within their own race. If 73% of black men are marrying within their own race, then obviously most black men do not marry white women. Since the stereotype asserts that successful black men are the ones who marry white women and I have no way of defining exactly what constitutes a successful black man, I will only assume that the numbers will still hold true at approximately 73%, even for the successful black men category.

The reason so many people accept the stereotype is that the media showcase celebrities and athletes who marry outside of their race and then exploit this point to make money. But the real question is, does it really matter? Does it really matter if a black man marries someone outside of his race? My immediate answer is no. I believe every person should have the right to choose who they want to marry and spend the rest of their lives with.

To insinuate that a black man only marries a white woman because of self-hatred or because he has a hatred of all black women is ludicrous in my opinion. Maybe, just maybe, he took the time to understand what qualities and values he was looking for in a woman and he happened to find them in a woman that happened to have a different color of skin.

I personally have no problem with interracial dating or marriage at all, and I believe the good news is that more and more people are becoming more open-minded and ultimately, we will realize that love knows no color. But to imply that black men aren't emotionally and intellectually competent in choosing their partners and only choose white women as a status symbol is an insult to black men.

Are there some black men who do? I'm sure there are, but I will assert that most of us are smart enough to know what we are looking for in a partner and we are willing to be open-minded in finding someone who meets our criteria.

Ultimately, the color of their skin shouldn't be the deciding factor. What matters most are the qualities and values the person holds true to and who they are on the inside, not the outside.

Which leads me to my final point. I often see articles and declarations about "black love". In my experience, there is really no such thing. Embracing this idea actually perpetuates the stereotype that we somehow love differently than other races and that is not the case. Love is love and it transcends race. It is the highest vibration and deepest feeling we experience as human beings. It comes from our ability to open our hearts and share the deepest, most intimate parts of ourselves with our partners. It is the ability to In-To-Me-See and our willingness to share what we see with the people we love. It is deeply spiritual and emotional and has absolutely nothing to do with our race. It's all about being human and sharing our humanness with another human being.

The beautiful thing about being human is we have this wonderful gift called choice: we get to choose who we love. Choose wisely.

Being a great father is not genetic. It is learned behavior. Therefore, every man can learn to become a great father regardless of what type of father he may have had.

Coach Michael Taylor

Illusion #7

Black Men Are Deadbeat Dads

In 2015, the OWN Network was scheduled to launch a reality show starring a man named Jay Williams. Mr. Williams' claim to fame was the fact that he had fathered 34 children by 17 different women. Fortunately, the backlash and outrage were so intense they canceled the show.

At a time when reality shows are so popular, it should come as no surprise that a network would even consider doing such a show. What surprised me was the fact that the OWN Network would even consider doing it. If this show had been released, it would have perpetuated the stereotype of black men being deadbeat dads. Although Mr. Williams could be considered as the epitome of irresponsible fathers, the fact that he happened to be a black male exacerbates the illusion that we aren't great fathers.

So, let's set the record straight. One of the most destructive illusions perpetuated by our media is that all black men are deadbeat dads. The ramifications of this illusion are devastating because this illusion tears at the very fabric of black male masculinity. It implies that we do not love or care for our children. It implies that we simply want to impregnate women and then have absolutely no responsibility or involvement with them once children are born.

Yet nothing could be further from the truth. We do love our children and the majority of us are actually pretty good fathers. To substantiate this, I would like to share a study done by the Center for Disease Control in 2013. In summary, the study found that black men were actually more involved with their children than other racial groups.

Here are a few statistics from the study. **More African-American fathers lived with their children** than living apart from their children, which contradicts the media-generated illusion that black men abandon their children. It also found that **78.2% fed or ate meals with their children** daily, compared with 73.9% of white fathers. The study also said **70.4% bathed, diapered, or dressed their children daily** compared with 60% of white fathers. It went on to say **82.2% play with their children daily and 34.9% read to their children** daily, compared with 24.9% of white fathers. **40.6% helped their children with their homework** or checked to make sure that they finished it daily compared with 29.3% of white fathers.

Of the fathers who live away from their children, African-American fathers outperform white and Latino fathers on nearly all major surveys, including reading for their children, helping them with their homework, and changing their diapers.

These are not statistics that you would normally see in mainstream media, but they do shed light on the fact that most black men are not deadbeat dads. The fact is we are no different than any other group of fathers.

It's important for us to understand that being a great father has nothing to do with genetics, it is learned behavior. If it is learned behavior, it means good habits can be learned and bad habits can be unlearned. A man who did not have a father figure or male role model in his life can still learn how to become a great father.

Although I did not have a great relationship with my father I made a choice that I was going to learn how to be a great father to my children. I actually remember the exact moment when I decided I was going to be a great dad.

When I was approximately 10 years old, I remember getting a spanking from my dad for something I didn't do. I remember feeling angry and hurt that my father refused to listen to what I had to say. At the time, the house we lived in was set on top of cinder blocks and I could crawl under the house beneath the concrete steps. This was my safe sacred space. It was my refuge when I felt sad, angry, or lonely. After the spanking, I felt all these emotions.

As I sat there under the steps thinking about my dad, I remember this exact thought: *"When I grow up, I'm not going to be like my father. I'm going to be a great dad."* I remember the thought as though it were yesterday. I still remember the anger and sadness I felt at the time and I remember an intuitive knowing that I was going to be a great father one day. That one simple thought set in motion everything I needed to become a great father.

Once I grew up and had children of my own, I remembered the promise I made to myself. So I read books, went to lectures, and took courses on being a great dad. As a result, I kept my promise to myself and I can say without hesitation that I became a great father. As a matter of fact, being a great dad is one of my proudest accomplishments.

To confirm this, I would like to share a post that my then 29-year-old daughter shared on Facebook for my 55th birthday.

It read: *"Great men aren't born great, they grow great! Today is the birthday of the best man in my life who has been the best father I could ever ask for. He motivates and inspires me, supports and loves me unconditionally. He is the most talented, driven and positive person I have ever known and I'm so very proud to have the privilege of calling this special one of a kind man my dad. Happy Birthday to a man who is truly great. I love you with all my heart and don't you ever forget it.*

Her post confirms what is most important to me, which is she loves her father and she knows that her father loves her. How often have you seen or heard that in the media from a black father? The truth is there are a lot of black fathers who can say the same thing, but it probably will not make the evening news. So, do not accept the stereotype that black men aren't great fathers. Instead, defy the stereotypes and become the absolute best father that you can possibly be.

With that being said, I would like to share my own experiences of becoming a father and how it positively impacted my life as a man.

I'll begin by sharing when I met my first wife and she already had an infant son. Although I was only 21 years old at the time, I was extremely mature for my age and fully understood the responsibilities of becoming a ready-made dad. Once we were married I knew that I wanted to adopt him and raise him as my own. As an adoptive father, it was never my intention to try to replace his biological father. I knew that my job was to love him and raise him to the best of my ability and make sure that he knew he was special to me. Therefore I had absolutely no problem telling him about his biological father and would actually support him if he wanted to have contact with him as he grew older. Adopting him and giving him my last name was a way for me to be connected to him and create an emotional bond that could never be broken. When the adoption papers went through and I was legally able to change his name to mine, in some ways it felt like giving birth to him. Although he was my son in my heart, having the official adoption papers and name change made it legal and binding and in some ways permanent in my heart.

Watching him grow up and become a confident, self-assured little boy was an absolute joy.

After a couple of years, my wife became pregnant with our first child. It was exciting and terrifying at the same time. Going through her pregnancy was a new experience and it was definitely something I had to learn to adapt to. I'll always remember her late night cravings for burritos and her crazy mood swings.

In August of 1983, hurricane Alicia headed directly for the gulf coast. As a manager of a building supply center, I was pulled in a million different directions. On top of that stress, my wife was just a few weeks away from delivering our baby. Without question, it was one of the most challenging times of my life. I was constantly worried about the challenges of managing a multi-million dollar business and I was also worried about ensuring that my wife and my child were going to be okay.

Thankfully everything worked out for the best and on September 12, 1983, my wife began having contractions and I knew it was the day that my first biological child would be born. On the way to the hospital, I was cool, calm, and collected. My wife, on the other hand, was a little nervous and concerned because she said it felt like the baby was already coming out as we were driving to the hospital.

By the time we got to the hospital the contractions had increased and the baby was ready to come out.

I pulled up to the emergency room entrance and ran inside to get a nurse and a wheelchair. It looked like a scene from a movie: frantic husband running through a hospital with a wheelchair screaming for people to get out of the way.

Once we were in the hospital they put my wife on a gurney and began wheeling her into the prep room. The doctor instructed me to go and put on the scrubs so I could join them in the operating room. I rushed into the bathroom and changed and headed to the operating room. When I got there (in less than three minutes) she wasn't there. Then a nurse ran in and grabbed my hand and said she was having the baby in the prep room. As I walked in, the doctor was delivering the baby and motioned for me to walk over and hold it.

Have you ever heard that having your first child will change your life? Well, I can definitely attest to this fact. As I stood there holding my son, it felt as if I went back in time and I was actually seeing my own birth. As I held him in my arms and he looked up and smiled at me it was as if I were looking at myself. The feeling of love was so powerful that it brought tears to my eyes. In that moment, I recognized that my son was a part of me and I had co-created this amazing human being. Words cannot come close to expressing the feeling I felt. Joy, excitement, gratitude, and love all rolled up into one emotion is the best way I can describe it.

Before he was born, my wife and I had decided on two different names to give him. We agreed to wait until he was born before we would decide. As I stared into his eyes and marveled at the miracle that he was, I knew that his named needed to be Michael. This was not one of the names we had chosen, but I knew I wanted to name him after me.

A couple of years later, my wife became pregnant with our second child. I had always wanted a daughter, so we decided to have another child in the hopes it would be a girl.

When the time came for my wife to have the baby it was a completely opposite experience from our first child. The first pregnancy was probably the easiest and fastest delivery ever.

From the moment she and I arrived at the hospital my son was born in less than 45 minutes!

However, this pregnancy was completely different.

My wife and I were sitting at home one evening and I noticed that her feet appeared to be swollen. When I asked her about it she said they were probably swollen because she had eaten too much salt that day. But something didn't seem right to me. They were simply *too* swollen. I decided to call the doctor because we were just a few days from the actual delivery date.

When I spoke to the doctor she told me to take her to the hospital immediately. Once we got there and they hooked her up to the EKG machines they found out that her blood pressure was abnormally high and she had an ailment called toxemia. The real problem we encountered was the medication that she needed to bring down her blood pressure would also bring down the baby's blood pressure and there was a possibility that one or both of them could actually die.

I felt so scared and helpless. There was nothing I could do. At the time, I was somewhat of an agnostic. I really didn't believe in God, but I wasn't completely closed minded to the idea that it could exist. I wasn't really comfortable praying, but I remember saying something to the effect of *"if you're real, please save my family."* Fortunately, my "prayers" were answered.

For two days the doctors struggled to bring down her blood pressure so they could deliver the baby. Finally, it was low enough for them to perform a C-section and my daughter was born healthy and my wife recovered just fine.

It's been said that fathers don't love their daughters more than their sons, they simply love them differently. I completely agree with this assertion. For me, I had always wanted a daughter. I've always believed that a father-daughter bond is a unique experience and having a "daddy's little girl" is something that a man cherishes differently than having a son. My relationship with my daughter confirms this and I feel blessed and grateful for the bond that we share.

Being a father was and is the highlight of my life. Watching my children grow up to be well-adjusted, happy individuals brings me great joy. Although I was a wonderful father, unfortunately, I fell short as a husband in a lot of ways. In retrospect, I can see how I neglected my role as a husband. I was so busy being a father and a manager I neglected my responsibilities as a husband and was not able to give my wife what she needed most. I take 100% responsibility for that neglect and my part in our marriage ending in divorce.

I'm a firm believer that everything happens for a reason. Although my divorce was difficult and painful at the time, the lessons I learned from it are invaluable and it is those very same lessons that have allowed me to now have a marriage that really works.

Since everything does happen for a reason, I recognize that my former wife was definitely a gift to me. She bore me two beautiful children and I will always love and respect her for the job she did raising them. Unlike some women, she recognized how important it was for our children to have access to their father. She never spoke negatively about me and she always made sure that I had access to my children. We had an extremely amicable divorce and were able to put our differences aside and do what was best for our children. I will always be indebted to her for her job as a mother.

As a father, I did the very best that I could, but I definitely made my share of mistakes. One of those mistakes was falling behind on child support.

After our divorce, I was trying to maintain two households on just my salary. At the time, the economy had taken a downturn and since I was paid on commission my salary decreased dramatically. Our divorce decree specified that I would pay her $750 per month. Since she didn't have a job and I was still living in our house, there was no way that I could afford to make the payments. Eventually, the house was foreclosed, and I filed for bankruptcy and moved into an apartment.

By now my divorce, bankruptcy, and foreclosure were taking their toll on me and I had become deeply depressed. I ended up quitting my job and spiraling deeper and deeper into debt and depression. Eventually, I became homeless and even considered taking my own life.

But the thing that kept me going was my children. I knew that I had to rebuild my life to not only get back on my feet but to also show my children that it was possible to overcome any adversity in your life.

Eventually, I was able to secure a job that allowed me to get back on my feet and begin rebuilding my life. This took several years and during that time I was still being charged $750 per month plus interest. I didn't know that I could have gone back to court and have that amount changed based on my current salary. So the interest and the debt continued to climb. At one point I was more than 50 thousand dollars behind on child support payments.

But that never stopped me from staying in touch with my kids. Although at times I was completely broke, I never missed my kids' birthdays or special occasions. At times I felt like a complete failure to my children but I never allowed my shame to keep me from staying in touch with them.

I'm happy to announce that I paid full restitution for every penny I owed in child support. It wasn't easy and it took several years, but I did it. I did it because it was my responsibility to do so. I did it because I owed it to my former wife and to my children. I did it because I am a man of integrity, and not paying it would have been out of character for me.

My point here is there are lots of black men who love and cherish their children. We are not deadbeat dads and most of us do the best we can despite the challenges we face.

As men who happen to be black, we must commit ourselves to being amazing fathers and make sure that we stay fully engaged in our children's lives. Our children should not be a burden on us, they must be the joy of our lives.

So be the father I know that you can be. Dispel the negative media stereotypes and show the world what an amazing father you are.

But most importantly, do it for you! Love your children and count your blessings to have them in your life. They are gifts from heaven, so treat them as such.

"People are dying in vain because America isn't holding their end of the bargain up, as far as giving freedom and justice, liberty to everybody. That's something that's not happening."

"I have great respect for the men and women that have fought for the USA. I have family, I have friends that have gone and fought for this country. And they fight for freedom, they fight for the people, they fight for liberty and justice, for everyone. That's not happening."

"There's people being murdered unjustly and not being held accountable. People are being given paid leave for killing people. That's not right. That's not right by anyone's standards."

"If we reach common ground, and can understand what everybody's going through, we can really affect change. And make sure that everyone is treated equally and has the same freedom."

- Colin Kaepernic

Illusion #8
Black Men Are Not Patriotic

Colin Kaepernick was a professional quarterback for the San Francisco 49ers. In response to several incidents of police brutality in America, in August 2016 he decided that he would not stand for the national anthem as a protest against the killings of innocent black men in America. In the beginning, he would sit during the anthem, which caused a major backlash for his protest. He was then accused of disrespecting the flag and insulting our military men and women.

After seeing Kaepernick's protest, ex-Green Beret Nate Boyer met with him and came up with a slight compromise to Colin sitting during the anthem. He convinced him that it would show more respect if he would simply take a knee instead of sitting. Colin agreed, and during the anthem, he would simply take a knee in silent protest to bring attention to an issue that he felt strongly about.

Since the protest began, it has become one of the most talked about topics in this country. Without question, there are strong feelings about this issue on both sides. Colin has been glorified and vilified for his protest, and I believe it has caused a much-needed conversation about police brutality in this country.

But unfortunately, the primary reason he began to protest has been distorted. The frenzy of media coverage has sadly diverted his primary message away from police brutality and focused it entirely on a black man who is disrespecting the flag and our military.

One of the reasons the media has focused on it being an issue of disrespecting the flag and our country is the result of a quote from the current president of the United States.

At a rally in Huntsville, Alabama, the president said:

> *"Wouldn't you love to see one of these NFL owners, when somebody disrespects our flag, to say, "Get that son of a bitch off the field right now. Out. He's fired. He's fired!" You know, some owner is going to do that. He's going to say, "That guy that disrespects our flag, he's fired." And that owner, they don't know it. They don't know it. They'll be the most popular person, for a week. They'll be the most popular person in this country."*

His comments galvanized his conservative base, who agreed with him and made the issue more about Colin disrespecting our flag and our military instead of focusing on the real issue of police brutality.

But his comments also triggered a wave of support for the protest as NFL owners and players showed solidarity and support by coming together the following week and joining the protest with locked arms, kneeling and raised fists.

Since my intention with this chapter is to dispel the illusion that black men aren't patriotic, I wanted to share an article I wrote in 2016 in response to Colin's protest. It was a featured article on the HuffPost website and it was my attempt to express my thoughts and feelings about this issue.

Is Colin Kaepernick Hurting or Helping Black Men in America?

As America continues to be divided by Colin Kaepernick's refusal to stand during the national anthem at his San Francisco 49ers football games, this story sheds light on the complexities of being a black man in America.

I'm reminded of a quote by Dr. Steven Covey from his bestselling book, The 7 Habits of Highly Effective People in which he stated, *"seek first to understand, and then be understood."* This quote truly captures how American society could address race relations going forward, and use Colin's protest as an opportunity for growth and transformation.

At first glance, it is understandable why so many people are upset about Colin not standing for the national anthem. To some, it appears that he is disrespecting the flag and his country. But if we are willing to look a little deeper and try to understand his motives, hopefully, it can change the perception of what he is attempting to do.

As I am reminded of the incidences of police brutality

against black men in this country, I can immediately empathize with Colin's protest. I can relate to his anger, frustration, and sadness about watching too many men of color needlessly lose their lives, and then have their perpetrators walk away without being held accountable for their actions. Understanding breeds compassion, and if we are willing to simply see this point of view, then we can recognize that this is the core of his protest. No matter how the media attempts to frame Colin's demonstration, I believe this is the primary reason he refuses to stand.

This leads us to the question: Is Colin's protest unpatriotic? Herein lies the great American hypocrisy. The dictionary defines a patriot as: *a person who vigorously supports their country and is prepared to defend it against enemies or detractors.* Isn't this exactly what Colin is attempting to do? He recognizes that American citizens are being killed and he is taking a stand against this crisis. How can this be viewed as unpatriotic? His actions are the highest form of patriotism. He is willing to not only sacrifice his livelihood for what he believes, he is actually willing to put his life on the line (he has received several death threats) in an attempt to make America better by bringing attention to the fact that too many men of color are being senselessly and unnecessarily killed.

According to Mike Freeman of Bleacher Report (www.bleacherreport.com), several NFL league officials actually hate Colin and his stance. Here are just a few quotes from top NFL officials: *"I don't want him anywhere near my team,"* one executive told Freeman. *"He's a traitor,"* said another exec. *"He has no respect for our country. F— that guy."* And from a general manager,

"In my career, I have never seen a guy so hated by front office guys as Kaepernick."

So, is it patriotic for a man to be hated simply because he is attempting to stop the killing of innocent Americans? Think about that for a moment.

In regards to the military, this is what they fight for. Service men and women fight for our right to speak out, defend our country, and use our freedom of speech to help improve this country. They aren't fighting for us to be silent when it comes to addressing issues within the confines of America. If we aren't willing to speak out to make America better, should that not be considered unpatriotic?

In a lot of ways, the Colin Kaepernick story is a microcosm of being a black man in America. On one hand, if we take a stand and speak out against social injustice, we are accused of being angry black men who hate America. On the other hand, if we aren't attempting to resolve the problems in our own communities, we are called lazy and indifferent to the challenges of black men in America.

As I've watched and listened to some of the opinions voiced by black men, I can only imagine how difficult it must be for Colin. There are some black men who attacked and vilified him for his stance while others embraced and supported his decision to protest. As a man who happens to be black, I can definitely relate to this conundrum. For most of my life, I have been accused of being a sellout because of my optimism and belief that nothing is impossible if you put your mind to it, even if you're black. I have been criticized, ostracized, and accused of being blind to the challenges facing black men in this country.

Sometimes it feels like a no-win situation. But you can't please everyone, so it's important to be clear on what you stand for and not be affected by the thoughts and opinions of others.

And now I would like to answer the question I posed at the beginning: Is Colin Kaepernick hurting or helping black men in America? I believe he is definitely helping black men, and more broadly, he is helping America. I say this because his actions have ignited a debate about police brutality and a few years from now, I believe he will be recognized and acknowledged for his willingness to take a stand (or in this case a knee) against an issue that has been pushed under the American rug for far too long. The time has come to face this challenge head on so that we cannot only eradicate police brutality but also bridge some of the racial divides in this country.

To be clear, I disagree with several of Colin's points in regards to this issue. But first and foremost, I completely agree with his right to protest, and I commend him for his courage to do so.

Thank you, Colin Kaepernick for teaching me that you do not necessarily have to stand up in order to love your country. You can kneel and love your country even when most people around you will accuse you of being a traitor.

~~~~~~~~~~~~

As an irrepressible optimist, I honestly believe that the challenges of race we are facing right now will eventually lead to unity and harmony. I realize that I am a minority in this way of thinking, but nevertheless that is what I believe.

Despite the apparent hatred and anger, we are bombarded with on a daily basis through our media, I still have faith in humanity that we will overcome these challenges.

With that being said, I wanted to speak directly to the CWBS.

I listened to a woman on social media who said if black men didn't like this country they should go back to their own. To which I reply, herein lies the biggest problem with the collective thinking of some white people. You must understand that America "is" our country, and we have every right to be here and call it our home. White people do not own this country, and they definitely do not have the monopoly on loving America, we love it too and we have earned the right to call it home. We love and appreciate this country more than you can possibly comprehend, despite the inhumane way we have been treated for as long as we've been here.

When we speak out against the injustices against us, we aren't saying we hate this country, we are saying that we love this country enough to want to make it better. If you don't have compassion and empathy for us when you see our children being senselessly killed in the streets that says more about you than it does about us. You need to know that our heart breaks when we see your children being killed by senseless acts of violence. We mourn your loss and feel your pain. When you see our young black males lose their lives unnecessarily to police violence do you feel our pain? Do you feel compassion for our loss? Or do you only see the media-generated stereotype and conclude that it's just another thug justifiably killed by a law-abiding police officer?

Have you ever had someone hate you simply for the color of your skin? Do you know what it feels like to be constantly invalidated by a system that sees you as less than human? Do you know what it feels like to see a burning cross and be reminded of how many of your people were murdered because of their skin pigmentation? Or how did you feel when a group of neo-Nazis paraded through Charlottesville Virginia with tiki torches shouting things like: *"Go the f--- back to Africa"* and *"F--- you, n-----!"*? Does it upset you to know that someone even shouted *"Dylann Roof was a hero!"* referring to the white supremacist who killed nine African Americans in a church in Charleston, S.C., in 2015.

And were you proud of your current president for not condemning the neo-Nazi's protest and indirectly supporting them by saying some of them were good people?

How do these events make you feel?

It's not my place to tell you what to feel, but I'm curious to know what you were thinking as you read the previous paragraphs. As men who happen to be black, we deal with these challenges on a daily basis. We also deal with the anger, rage, sadness, fear, and confusion of being a minority in a country that has primarily been majority white. If you could take a walk in our shoes, I'm certain you would feel differently.

But despite the hostility and rejection we've experienced for years, we continue to hold on to the dream of being accepted as equals. And unfortunately, we will never be seen as equals if we do not speak out about the injustices and unfairness we are exposed to on a daily basis.

Our protests aren't about hate. They're about love. Love of self and love of country. Every great movement that has changed this country for the better began as a simple protest. The civil rights movement would never have started without protest. The women's rights movement would never have started without protest. The gay rights movement would never have happened without protest. Each of these movements was started by some courageous people who chose to make America better by their protests.

To help you better understand the difficulty of being a black man in America, I want to use the story of Jesse Owens as a metaphor. In case you've forgotten or never heard of Jesse Owens, he was the black track and field star who won four gold medals at the 1936 Olympics.

During that time, Adolf Hitler was boasting about white supremacy and he made several comments saying Germans were the ultimate superior race and no one could beat them in the Olympic competition.

Now try to imagine what it must have been like for Jesse Owens. His country was asking him to be a representative for America and go to Germany to compete against the Germans. He knew that the Germans would hate him, yet he believed it was his civic and personal duty to race despite the opposition. There were some black people who believed he shouldn't go because of the way black people were being treated in America at the time. I can only imagine the conflict he must have felt choosing between staying home to speak out against racism and going to Germany to also confront racism, but this time from Germans, not Americans. But Jesse knew that it was his patriotic duty to represent his country and he chose to go to the Olympics.

During the 1936 Olympics, Jesse Owens single-handedly obliterated Hitler's assertion about Germans being the superior race. Not only did he win four Gold medals, he also set three World records and tied another. (If you have not watched the movie Race that showcases Jesse Owens story I highly recommend that you do).

Now try to imagine how Jesse Owens must have felt in winning those gold medals for his country and setting those world records. I can only imagine just how proud he must have felt to have shown the world what an amazing athlete he was, but even more importantly what a great American athlete he was.

Of course, America was struggling with race relations at that time and it must have been extremely difficult for Jessie to come home to America and still have to deal with the anger, racism, and discrimination that was so prevalent at that time. Despite the fact that he won four gold medals as a representative of the United States of America, he was still viewed as inferior and less than human by the majority of white people in America.

Jesse's story is a metaphor and a microcosm of being a black man in America. No matter what we may contribute or how much we love our country, too many times we are viewed as unpatriotic and undeserving to be American.

And yet my optimism remains. My optimism remains because of people like Colin Kaepernick who are courageous enough to take a stand for something they believe in. I'm optimistic because of people like Nate Boyer, who took the time to fully understand the reason for Colin's protest and then partner with him to find some common ground in the hopes of bringing people together.

I'm optimistic because of the NFL owners and athletes who have supported the protest and not allowed the current president's words to keep them from standing together as a team.

I'm optimistic because of the men and women of our military who recognize that the protest was never about disrespecting them or the flag and they have chosen to take a knee with Kaepernick.

I'm also optimistic because of the people who disagree with me and my views about the protest. Not the few racists who are making their decisions based on hate. But for the people who really do love this country and are doing what they believe is right by disagreeing with the protest.

This is what makes America great! The diversity of thought and belief and the willingness to agree to disagree and not make other people feel they're wrong when they disagree with you.

Herein lies the solution to all of our problems.

So let's agree to disagree. Let's be willing to see other points of view. Let's keep our hearts and minds open and do not make other people wrong because of their point of view. Hold firmly to what you truly believe and allow others to do the same without attack or criticism. Once we do that then America can heal and move forward.

In the meantime, take a knee and love your country.

"Herein lies the tragedy of the age: not that men are poor—all men know something of poverty; not that men are wicked—who is good? Not that men are ignorant—what is truth? Nay, but that men know so little of men."

- W.E.B. Du Bois
The Souls of Black Folk

Illusion #9

Black Men Are Physically/Sexually Superior

There are few things in this country that has brought more pride to black people than athletes - from Jesse Owens to Usain Bolt, Muhammad Ali to Mike Tyson, Wilt Chamberlain to LeBron James, Jim Brown to Le'Veon Bell, Jackie Robinson to Barry Bonds - black athletes have always been symbols of progress and pride. Their struggles uplift us, challenge us, motivate and inspire us. Through them we see possibilities. Through them we see success.

Whenever I felt discouraged and felt like giving up, I would think about people like Jackie Robinson. I tried to imagine how difficult it must have been for him to be a black baseball player at a time when he must have felt like the whole world was against him. Not only was he dealing with the external hatred from the fans, he also had to deal with the internal hatred from his own teammates. How was he able to do that? How did he not succumb to the rage and hatred he must have felt on and off the field on a daily basis?

Although there are no easy answers to these questions, I'd like to think the reason he was able to do so was because of his love of baseball. Jackie was born to play baseball. He loved the sport so much that he was willing to deal with all the adversity and opposition he encountered on a regular basis. By focusing on the game he loved, he was able to overcome a multitude of challenges, and in doing so he paved the way for others to follow in his footsteps.

This is why athletes and sports are so important, especially to black people. Their stories of overcoming adversity teach us the importance of focusing on our passions and purpose, and not allowing anything to keep us from living our dreams. In order to become a professional athlete, a person must have vision, commitment, patience, perseverance, and focus. These qualities are what allow an average person to become an *extraordinary* person, and that is what inspires us. It inspires us because it lets us know that nothing is impossible when you set your mind to it.

If you watch major sports like basketball, football, and track & field, it's easy to accept the stereotype that black men are physically superior to other races. But is this something that is scientifically verifiable? Believe it or not, the answer is no. Without question, black men do excel in these specific sports, but in no way does it prove that we are somehow physically superior to other races.

Whenever a specific group attempts to prove its superiority, it automatically invalidates all other groups, so our goal should not be to prove that we are better than other groups -

it should be to make sure that we are not shown to be less than, but equal to all of them.

To make a point, let's look at some numbers. In pro football, there are 32 teams and they are allowed to have 53 players on their rosters. This equates to 1696 players. In pro basketball, there are 30 teams with an average of 15 players per team, which equates to 450 players. In major league baseball, there are 30 teams comprised of 25 players, which totals 750 players. When we take the three major sports in America and add them up, we get a total of 2,896 athletes.

Think about that total for a minute. **There are only 2,896 highly paid pro athletes playing these three sports!** Athletes make up a minuscule fraction of men in America, and it isn't feasible to assume that one race of men is superior to the other. What you are seeing is the best of the best. The elitists. To become one, you have to be extraordinary. So let's celebrate our athletes and be inspired by their efforts, but do not accept the stereotype that we are in any way superior to other men.

Another media-generated illusion is that black men are sexually superior to other men. On the surface, this may appear to be a compliment, but in reality, it isn't. In a society that lives by the motto, *sex sells*, it's no wonder men in general struggle with sexuality. Our media constantly bombards us with images of beautiful half-naked women and the unconscious belief that as men our job is to simply sleep with as many of them as possible.

The media-generated stereotype of all black men being *hung to their knees* and that they are sexually superior places a lot of pressure on black men and it makes it difficult for any black man to feel like he measures up (pun intended).

The downside to this is that some black men feel inadequate and inferior if they can't live up to the stereotype. In rare cases, this insecurity can lead to all types of negative behavior, including rape and domestic violence.

Without question, this stereotype is exacerbated by the over-proliferation of sexual messages through our media and our culture. When we watch or hear stories about celebrities or athletes *making it rain* at strip clubs and spending thousands of dollars watching women shake their naked bodies for men's pleasure, unconsciously we begin to associate masculinity with sex. It then reinforces the idea that men gain their identities from their ability to perform sexually.

So, let's set the record straight: there is no scientific evidence that supports the idea that black men are sexually superior to any other race of men. We aren't all hung to our knees and we definitely believe in lovemaking versus just physical sex (although there is absolutely nothing wrong with physical sex in the right context). We are capable of creating intimate encounters with our partners that include emotional, physical, intellectual, and spiritual connection, and we understand the importance of affection and appreciation in our relationships.

What's been missing for us as black men is our willingness to engage in a dialog about the importance of intimacy and connection versus physical sex. It's easy for us to pound our chest and brag about our sexual conquests, but it is extremely difficult to be real and authentic about our true feelings and emotions.

In order for us to transcend the media stereotypes about our sexuality, we must be willing to educate ourselves about our emotions and sexual desires. It is my experience that as black people we seldom speak openly about these things. I'm sure some of this could be attributed to our reliance on religion, which in too many cases is the source of our sexual dysfunction because of the shame and guilt some religions create. But since you and I are having this open conversation, let's tackle this issue head-on.

So let's begin with an open, honest question. Take some time to think about it before you answer. When you do, make sure that you're being completely honest with yourself.

Are you currently happy with your sex life? Are you honestly, completely 100% satisfied with your sex life?

What's your answer?

Write it here: _____

Let's do a simple exercise. On a scale of 1–10, how happy are you with your sex life right now? One means you are completely unhappy and ten means you are extremely happy.

Write your answer here: _____

If you didn't answer with a 10, ask yourself *why not?* What is it that is keeping you from being 100% satisfied with your sex life?

Write your answer here: _____

Maybe your answer is that you currently don't have a partner. Or maybe you have a partner and you aren't having enough sex. Or maybe you're having enough sex but it isn't fulfilling and something seems to be missing.

No matter what your answer is, I can assure you that the key to being completely happy with your sex life has very little to do with the physical act of sex. The key to being 100% happy with your sex life is to ensure that you have intimacy and connection in your relationship. Without it, there is no way that you will ever be fully satisfied.

Why is that? Because we have been conditioned to believe that sex is primarily a physical act when in reality, making love is an emotional and spiritual act. When you lack emotional intimacy in relationships, it seldom satisfies you. Of course, it can bring you some temporary pleasure, but it is always short term. If you want long-term connection and mind-blowing sex, you have to combine the emotional and the spiritual with the physical.

This is the reason it's so important for you to take the time to do your emotional healing work. You must be willing to get in touch with all of your emotions if you truly want to experience intimacy with another person. If you have unresolved emotional conflict from childhood trauma or have had bad experiences from previous relationships, the chances are you have emotional scars that need to be healed. You must be willing to heal those scars before you can create emotionally healthy relationships.

This is by far the greatest challenge we have as men of color. Most of us are simply unwilling to admit that we have issues and emotional healing to do. But the only way out is through. You must be willing to go through your own healing process and get in touch with your emotions if you want to create great relationships that include great sex.

I'd like to share an article written by a guy named Bernardo Mendez titled **5 Tips To Deepen Your Sexual Connection With Your Partner** and it is a very well-written article that touches on the topic of intimacy.

Be sure to read it slowly and carefully, and take notes of any thoughts and feelings you might have as you read it.

> When you think about having sex, would you say "intimacy" is the first thing that comes to your mind? Do you think of sex as a place to feel truly seen, loved and free to fully express yourself?
>
> If you're finding yourself answering "no" to any or most of these questions, you're not alone. For most (honest) people, the answer to it is a resounding "no."
>
> But why? Especially given that sex is, basically by definition, one of the purest expressions of intimacy there is. Yet throughout my many years of coaching women and couples to connect more deeply to love and desire, I've noticed a huge gap between what most people truly long for in sex and what they actually experience in their day-to-day lives.

Because this gap creates a great deal of suffering, disappointment, resentments and other unpleasant emotions, I want to share five tips with you about how to deepen your experience of intimacy in the bedroom. With these essential keys in mind, you can begin to focus on radically clarifying your desires when it comes to sex and intimacy. By getting in touch with your expectations, and those of your partner, you can begin to make sex into a practice that really and truly prioritizes the art of intimacy.

1. Recognize the importance of cultivating an intimate friendship with your partner.

Many people who want to feel deeply connected during sex (who doesn't?!) tend to focus too much on technique — the details of sex itself. In reality, however, the quality of your relationship with your partner is far more important for feeling intense intimacy in the bedroom.

Emotional connection, mutual trust and a sense of safety within the relationship can basically be thought of as a prerequisite to the fulfillment of your sexual desires. Intimacy also requires acceptance, understanding and, of course, physical attraction. Ultimately, it's that feeling of being at home with someone that we crave so much, and that makes the actual act of sex so pleasurable.

One of the most underrated ways to increase trust and ditch fear in your relationship (which hinders intimacy during sex) is to really work on developing a solid, always-evolving friendship with your partner. When your relationship is a safe space to share, be and express without being judged, your ability to offer more and surrender without reservations in the bedroom greatly increases.

2. Connect deeply to your own body.

The everyday stressors of life — from work to cleaning our houses to making dinner to paying bills — keep most of us from maintaining consistent and thorough self-care routines. A result of this is that most of us devote a minimal amount of time to exploring, embracing and enjoying our own bodies.

Unfortunately, these effects of stress trickle down into our sex lives. When we haven't developed a comfortable and intimate relationship with ourselves, it's nearly impossible to cultivate a comfortable and intimate sexual relationship with someone else.

When you create the space to feel, explore and love your own body, you are better able to communicate what you want, what you crave and what makes you feel fulfilled.

3. Speak up!

One of the most common reasons that sex starts to feel routine, and far less passionate, is through lack of communication. This is essential to keep in mind for intimacy in the bedroom, but also outside of the bedroom. Ask yourself, Am I expressing my authentic truth in my relationship? Or are you hiding from yourself, and your partner, in order to keep the peace?

It might seem like overreacting if you want to voice how pissed you felt when your partner looked at your friend with flirty eyes. It may seem unnecessary to express how disappointed you were when your partner didn't really acknowledge your effort in planning the perfect date. But think about it this way: when you suppress your pain in one moment, it doesn't go away; it will simply come up again, in another form.

One of the ways this happens is through suppressed intimacy — emotionally, sexually and beyond. The more you can practice shortening the time it takes between feeling hurt and letting the other person know, the lower your chances of developing resentment. Less resentment and other negativity mean a greater willingness to give and receive in other ways, especially when it comes to sex. So speak up!

4. Embrace the light, the dark, and the gradations in between.

Many couples fall into the trap of sexual monotony over time. Unsurprisingly, this monotony often coexists with a sense of safety — and feeling safe with your partner is a good thing. Yet widening the range of expressiveness can be a doorway to the deepest spiritual connection between two humans, and that often involves stepping a bit outside the safety zone (in a variety of ways).

Maybe expressing your fears about something in your relationship strike you as "bad," something to avoid. Well, stepping outside the safety zone, and embracing your "dark" parts may be exactly what you, and the relationship, needs in order to feel greater intimacy. In the bedroom, this might take the form of allowing your partner to take you with more strength and abandon or for you to express a deeper degree of hunger, sensuality, vulnerability and openness in your desires.

If you allow yourself to explore your fantasies without shame and surrender more fully into your deepest desires, you can proactively add a depth of experience, unlike anything you've ever felt.

5. Surrender to the outcome.

So much of the disconnection that arises during intimacy can be traced down to a pressure to perform or achieve something. Whether that is having an orgasm, trying to look a certain way or being perceived as a gifted lover, it distracts from the sacredness and beauty of the present moment.

What if the entire outcome was to experience your partner — in the moment — and offer something deeply yours to him or her? If you didn't feel pressured to reach a milestone during intimacy, how much deeper could you let go, enjoy and surrender to your partner?

When we can use sex as an expression of love, service and presence, we open the doorway to experiencing sex as a spiritual experience too.

Most human beings will use intimacy as a way to experience release or feel pleasure; few will have the courage to really get into someone's heart. But those who have to courage to do so will have a fulfilling depth in life unlike anything they might have imagined.

~~~~~~~~~~~~~

Well, what did you think as you read the article? Did it

resonate with you? Did you agree with it? Did you even read it?

I have come to know that great relationships are contingent upon intimacy and connection. It all begins with our willingness to learn to love ourselves and then being willing to share ourselves with others. This takes an incredible amount of courage and vulnerability, which too many times terrifies most men. But since you've come this far, I'm absolutely certain that you can create the relationship of your dreams.

So make sure that you go against the media stereotype of black men and commit to creating true intimacy and connection in your own life. In doing so, you will be joining my revolution of empowering black men to live extraordinary lives.

Welcome to the revolution!

"Wanna fly, you got to give up the shit that weighs you down."

- Toni Morrison
Song of Solomon

Illusion #10

Black Men Are Lazy

I love that quote from Toni Morrison: *"Wanna fly, you got to give up the shit that weighs you down."* So, what is the *shit* that's weighing you down? I believe it is holding on to negative beliefs and stereotypes about black men. In other words, it's your mindset that keeps you trapped in mediocrity and keeps you from flying.

One of the most debilitating and disempowering stereotypes about black men is that we're lazy. We've all seen the negative images of brothers hanging out on corners shooting dice or hanging around the playground and doing nothing but playing basketball.

The negative images are endless, and unfortunately far too many black men fall victim to this stereotype. Instead of blaming the CWBS or the media, I want to focus my attention on ways you can avoid falling into the trap of complacency and non-action.

So, are you truly ready to give up the *shit that weighs you down* in order for you to fly?

If the answer is yes, let's begin with this question: **Are you optimistic or pessimistic about your future?**

Choose one: Optimistic ~ Pessimistic

It's important for you to know that your attitude will definitely determine your altitude. Henry Ford said it best when he stated: *"Whether you believe you can or whether you believe you can't, you will always be right."*

My suggestion is, make sure you begin with an optimistic outlook. I know this may be difficult to do with all of the negativity and pessimism of our media, but it is absolutely imperative that you incorporate an optimistic mindset if you truly want to be successful in any area of your life.

I'm going to share something with you to help you get started. It's from one of my previous books, **Adversity Is Your Greatest Ally ~ How To Use Life Challenges As Stepping Stones To Live The Life Of Your Dreams.** I'm also going to suggest that you pick up a copy of the book for yourself and drink in the wisdom I share. You can also gain FREE access to a powerful live presentation I gave based on the presentation I'm about to share with you. To gain access, simply log on to www.adversityisyourgreatestally.com

To make sure that you are no longing holding on to the shit that is weighing you down, I want to share my *5 Keys To Turn Your Adversity Into Allies.* These are the same 5 keys I have used to overcome all the challenges in my life, and if you are willing to incorporate them into your own I am absolutely certain they will help you fly.

Key 1: You must be willing to take 100 percent responsibility for your life.

That's it! If you are unwilling to do this you might as well stop reading this book right now. Your success relies on your willingness to take 100 percent responsibility for your life and everything that happens to you. You can't blame your parents, where you were born, or the color of your skin. You can't blame your lack of education, your ex-spouse, or your age. **You** must decide that you're going to take 100 percent responsibility for your life, and then make it happen.

Are you willing to do this?

Of course, this does not mean that there won't be people who may hurt you, lie to you, or betray you. It does not mean that there won't be times when you are tired, frustrated, angry, confused, and simply want to give up. It also doesn't mean that there won't be times where you might try to place blame on the government, society, religion, or the particular culture you were brought up in for being the cause of your failure.

It means you are making a conscious decision, right now, that you are willing to do whatever it takes, and you recognize that if you do not assume 100 percent responsibility for your life, you literally give up your power.

A good way to do this is to remember the Three C's. Choice, Chance, and Change. It all begins with you first and foremost making the choice that you will take 100 percent responsibility for your life to turn out the way you want it to. And then you must make the choice to take the chance that you can then change your life.

Of course, this takes some risk, but with huge risk comes huge reward, and you must take a chance if you want anything in your life to change.

Make the choice to take a chance if you want your life to change. **Choose right now!**

So, that's the first key to turn adversities into allies: **Take 100 percent responsibility for your life.**

Key 2: You must be willing to get out of your comfort zone.

Another way to look at getting out of your comfort zone is simply being willing to face your fears. It's been said that fear is the destroyer of dreams, and if you aren't willing to address your fears, you will never be able to accomplish anything of significance.

There is a wonderful quote that states: "You must realize, that fear is not real. It is a product of thoughts you create. Do not misunderstand me, danger is very real, but fear is a choice."

Fear is a choice. You can choose to let it keep you from accomplishing your goals, or you can feel the fear and do it anyway. A powerful acronym for fear is False Experiences Appearing Real, which means they are simply thoughts in your mind that appear to be real, yet, they are simply figments of your imagination. They only exist within the framework of your own mind. Getting out of your comfort zone means you learn to recognize your fears, and don't let them stop you from accomplishing your goals.

Getting out of your comfort zone means being willing to be uncomfortable. As a matter of fact, you must learn to become comfortable with being uncomfortable, if you truly want to accomplish extraordinary things in your life.

Key 3: You must commit to your own personal growth.

As a human being you have an infinite capacity for learning, and if you're not willing to learn, no one can help you; but if you are determined to learn, no one can stop you either. It is absolutely imperative that you make a commitment to growth. There's a wonderful saying that goes, "If you aren't growing, you're dying." So make a commitment to constant and never-ending improvement, and I can assure you, you'll be able to turn your adversities into allies.

Another way to look at growth is using the computer as a metaphor for your brain. A computer is an amazing technological machine that can be used to do remarkable things. To improve the performance of a computer you must constantly upgrade software and replace hardware to keep it running at its maximum potential. Your brain is more powerful than any computer, and you must be willing to constantly upgrade your internal software and take care of your hardware to keep it, too, running at its maximum potential.

Upgrading your inner software means that you are willing to look at the subconscious beliefs that may be limiting your potential. It also means that you are willing to add new programs (beliefs) that can support you in your growth. You can accomplish this by reading books and participating in classes that provide you with the knowledge to accomplish your goals and support you in feeling better about yourself as a human being.

The key is to commit to constant and never-ending improvement in all areas of your life.

Key 4: You must develop a positive attitude.

So what exactly is attitude? My definition of attitude is, "The compilation and expression of your beliefs, thoughts, and feelings."

If you have negative beliefs, thoughts, and feelings, you're going to have a negative attitude. If you have positive beliefs, thoughts, and feelings, you're going to have a positive attitude. So if you're truly committed to turning your adversities into allies, one of the things you have to do is to develop a positive attitude; because whenever life throws challenges at you, if you have a negative attitude, guess what happens? It's going to make things more difficult for you to deal with. But, if you maintain a positive attitude, and if you maintain the idea that it is absolutely possible for you to overcome challenges in your life, then it's going to be much easier for you to turn your adversities into allies. Developing a positive mental attitude is paramount to your success.

Key 5: You must discover your unique gifts and talents.

Whether you believe this or not, you have very special unique gifts and talents. Chances are, you have forgotten what they are, and more than likely you've given up on sharing them with the world - but rest assured they are within you. Your goal is to discover these gifts and talents and reignite the inner flame of passion that will allow you to express them. Your gifts are not necessarily something you do - they are primarily about who you are. For example, being loving and caring is a gift. Being intelligent and analytical is also a gift. Being ambitious, driven, creative and extroverted, or being introverted and compassionate is a gift.

When you discover your gifts and apply them to your talents, then you will find your true purpose in life. If your gifts are being loving and caring, then your talent could lead you to be a healer or a member of the clergy. If your gifts include being intelligent and analytical, then your talent could lead you to become a doctor or a lawyer. If your gifts include being ambitious and driven, then you may become an entrepreneur or a manager. If you are creative and extroverted, chances are you will become some type of entertainer, and if you are introverted and compassionate, then you may choose to become a therapist or counselor.

Get the picture?

Your gifts are lying dormant within you. It is your responsibility to wake them up. No one can discover or express them for you, you must commit to discovering them for yourself. When you do, I can assure you that you will not only be able to fully express yourself authentically, but you will also be able to find joy and passion in everything you do.

Find your gifts and express your talents and you can live a rewarding life.

~~~~~~~~~~~~

Now I would like to share a quote from Jim Rohn: *"You are the average of the five people you spend the most time with."* So take a moment right now and ask yourself, *who are the five people I spend the most time with?* As a matter of fact, let's write them down right now.

1. _____

2. _____

3. _____

4. _____

5. _____

As you review your list, I want you to notice a few things about the people on it. Are they honest? Are they intelligent? Are they successful? Are they positive? Do they encourage you to be better?

This exercise isn't about judging your friends or telling you who you should hang out with. The intention is for you to recognize who they are and how they act and then be willing to ask yourself if they add value to your life or if they take value away.

It's vital for you to recognize how important the people you surround yourself with are. Whether you admit it or not, these people strongly influence your behavior and life.

I would now like to know if you've ever heard of the following men: Dr. Mohammed Ibrahim, Patrice Motsepe, Robert Smith, and Mike Adenuga. Have you heard of any of these men before? Do you know what they all have in common?

The common thread is they are each black men who happen to be billionaires. That's right, billionaire with a b!

If you want to be successful, it's important that you hang around with successful people. Although you may not be able to physically hang out with them, you can do so by reading their books, visiting their websites, listening to their audio programs, and interacting with them on social media. There is no excuse not to learn from the people who you are trying to emulate. It's also important for you to remember that you should not limit yourself to just stories about black men. If there is something that you're passionate about and dream about it doesn't matter what color your teachers and mentors are. Simply find the men and women who inspire you, and follow and learn from them.

One of my dreams is to become a billionaire, so I study people like Jeff Bezos, Elon Musk, Peter Diamandis, Warren Buffet, and the black men I mentioned earlier. I learn as much as I can from them so that I can gain the knowledge to follow in their footsteps.

Remember, success has no color except green if you want to be an entrepreneur. Even if you don't have dreams to be a billionaire, it's important you follow the people who are doing the things you want to do.

So in summary, you must begin with an **optimistic mindset** then follow the **5 keys to turn your adversity into allies** and make sure the five people you spend the most time with are adding value to your life instead of taking it away. Commit to learning from the people who are doing what you want to do.

There are no limits to what you can accomplish. The only limits you have are the ones that you place on yourself. Be sure to let go of the shit that is weighing you down and allow yourself to fly. When you do this, you will automatically eradicate the illusion that black men are lazy.

It's time for you to fly!

~~~~~~~~~~~~

So, there you have them - the ten most destructive media-generated illusions about black men. Once you learn to recognize them and not act consistently with them, I can assure you that you've laid the groundwork for creating a life of your dreams.

Let's review them one more time to make sure that you ground them deep into your psyche and ensure you **wake up** from them and not **become** them.

Illusion #1 ~ Black Men Are an Endangered Species

Illusion #2 ~ Black Men Use Race As an Excuse for Failure

Illusion #3 ~ Black Men Try To Be White

Illusion #4 ~ Black Men Are Less Intelligent

Illusion #5 ~ Black Men Are Angry and Violent

Illusion #6 ~ Black Men Cannot Be Monogamous

Illusion #7 ~ Black Men Are Deadbeat Dads

Illusion #8 ~ Black Men Are Not Patriotic

Illusion #9 ~ Black Men Are Sexually/Physically Superior

Illusion #10 ~ Black Men Are Lazy

In summary, black men are **not** an endangered species and we do **not** use race as an excuse for failure. We are aware of the multiplicity of challenges we are faced with, yet we maintain our identity and never attempt to be someone or something we are not. We recognize our brilliance and are committed to expanding our minds and intellects. We are in touch with all of our emotions, and we are committed to being as real and authentic as we can be as we express them. We create and maintain loving, rewarding, fulfilling, and monogamous relationships that nurture and support us and we make them high priorities in our lives. We love, honor, and nurture our children to become healthy and happy individuals that become our legacy for generations to come. We take care of our physical bodies and are comfortable with our sexuality in whatever form it takes. We maintain excellent work habits and ethics and create extraordinary lives that fulfill and sustain us.

My hope is that this book has shined the light of truth on the illusion that black men are in any shape, form or fashion an endangered species. I will assert again that I believe we are positioned for unprecedented levels of success in the future and I hope this book has given you some tools of awareness that will assist you in your personal growth and development.

If you are inspired by this message and want to do your part in changing the negative media-generated narrative about black men, my suggestion is that you share this book with as many people as possible. Start conversations about it. Buy copies for your relatives and friends. Share it on social media. Do whatever you can to spread its positive message so that men of color create a new wave of optimism and possibilities for the future.

But most importantly, wake up from these illusions and create the life you were born to live. **You are 100% responsible for your life.** Take control of it and create the life of your dreams.

Coach Michael Taylor

About the Author

Coach Michael Taylor is an entrepreneur, author, motivational speaker, and radio show host who has dedicated his life to empowering men and women to reach their full potential. He knows first-hand how to overcome adversity and build a rewarding and fulfilling life and he is sharing his knowledge and wisdom with others to support them in creating the life of their dreams.

He is no stranger to adversity and challenges. He was born in the inner-city projects of Corpus Christi Texas to a single mother with six children. Although he dropped out of high school in the 11th grade, his commitment to living an extraordinary life supported him in defying the odds.

With persistence, patience, and perseverance, he was able to climb the corporate ladder of success and become a very successful mid-level manager of a multi-million-dollar building supply center at the tender young age of 21. After approximately eight years, he was then faced with another set of challenges as he experienced the pain and humiliation of divorce, bankruptcy, and foreclosure and found himself contemplating suicide.

Bankrupt and alone, he committed to rebuilding his life which propelled him to begin a 20-year inner journey of personal transformation which resulted in him discovering his true self and his passions for living. As a result, he is now happily married (14 years) and living his dream of living an extraordinary life while being in service to others. Through his books, lectures, and radio program, he now coaches others on how to become genuinely happy with their lives and live the lives they were born to live.

www.coachmichaeltaylor.com
www.adversityisyourgreatestally.com
www.creationpublishing.com
www.anewconversationwithmen.com
www.bmracademy.com

Contact us:
Email: mtaylor@coachmichaeltaylor.com
Phone: 877-255-3588

CPSIA information can be obtained
at www.ICGtesting.com
Printed in the USA
BVHW01s1107280118
506531BV00023B/713/P